ALAN DUNN'S
Celebration Cakes

ALAN DUNN'S
Celebration Cakes

Read. Learn. Do What You Love.

Published 2017 — IMM Lifestyle Books
www.IMM LifestyleBooks.com

IMM Lifestyle Books are distributed in the United Kingdom by Grantham Book Services,
Trent Road, Grantham, Lincolnshire, NG31 7XQ.

In North America, IMM Lifestyle Books are distributed by Fox Chapel Publishing,
1970 Broad Street, East Petersburg, PA 17520, www.FoxChapelPublishing.com.

ISBN   978-1-5048-0075-4

10 9 8 7 6 5 4 3 2 1

Printed in Singapore

For Andrew, Avril, Allen and Sue

This book is not only about celebration cakes and flowers, it is also a celebration of the friendships and working relationships built over the last 15 years of writing books! I really don't know where I would have been without the never-ending supply of help, support and kindness from the following who have been such a huge help with this title in too many ways to mention in this small space! A huge thank you to Sue Atkinson, Corinne Masciocchi, Edyta Girgiel, Sathyavathi Narayanswamy, Alice Christie, Alex Julian, Tombi Peck, Maria Harrison, Jen and Pea, Conor Day, Tony Warren, John Quai Hoi, Andrew Lockey and last but not least my folks!

Contents

Introduction

My interest in cake decorating was fuelled at an early age – my grandfather was a baker and although he had retired by the time I had taken a real interest, the seeds had already been planted. But it was only later on in my teens that I started developing ideas and designs for what I think of as proper celebration cakes.

In December 1986 I decorated my very first Christmas cake – this was not a particularly impressive design and the royal iced coating was so badly executed that it was almost impossible to cut through – but it spurred me on to seek cake decorating books from both the school and public libraries. A few months later I discovered some magical books – they contained beautifully designed and executed sugarpaste-coated cakes decorated with sugar flowers. It was then that I realised cake decorating was going to play a major part in my life. The next opportunity I had to design a celebration cake was for Mother's Day. I decorated the cake with simple hand-modelled sugarpaste roses – this endeavour was much more successful than the previous year's Christmas cake attempt and really marked the starting point for my interest and passion for making sugar flowers. The next cake I worked on was for my grandparents' diamond anniversary – a bell-shaped cake with hand-moulded roses. It was around this time that I attended my first sugar flower class and joined The British Sugarcraft Guild. It was through these classes and monthly guild branch meetings that I realised that sugar flowers could be taken to another level.

This book is a celebration of cakes, flowers, fruit, vegetables and the odd nut too! Flowers and cakes have proved to be a successful combination for centuries and for me too they are a real motivation to strive to create interesting floral designs for any occasion. For years I have included berries, fruits and nuts into my work and for the first time I am now creating vegetables, which are proving to be a really fun addition.

Here, I have tried to create designs that are ideal as impressive centrepieces for most of the major celebrations in life. Many of the cake themes are interchangeable to make them appropriate for other occasions, and hopefully the variety of designs will help you to create an individual style of your own too!

Alan Dunn

EQUIPMENT AND MATERIALS

There is a huge array of sugarcraft equipment and materials commercially available. Here, a variety of items that I consider to be very useful are listed.

EQUIPMENT

Non-stick board

This is an essential addition to the flower-maker's workbox. Avoid white boards as they strain the eyes too much. Some boards can be very shiny, making it difficult to frill the petals against them. If this is the case, simply roughen up the surface using some fine glass paper prior to use or turn over the board and use the back, which is often less shiny. I always apply a thin layer of white vegetable fat rubbed into the surface of the board, then remove most of the excess with dry kitchen paper – this stops the paste sticking to the board and also makes you check each time to see if it is clean from food colour.

Rolling pins

It's good to have a selection of non-stick rolling pins in various sizes. They are essential for rolling out flowerpaste, sugarpaste and almond paste successfully.

Foam pads

Foam pads are ideal to place petals and leaves on while you soften the edges – especially if you have hot hands that tend to dissolve the petals as you are working them. Prior to buying this product, check that it has a good surface as some have a rough-textured surface that will tear the edges of your petals or leave marks on them. I either prefer the large blue pad called a Billy's block or the yellow celpad.

Wires and floristry tape

I buy mostly white paper-covered wires, preferring to colour or tape over as I work. The quality varies between brands. The most consistent in quality are the Japanese Sunrise wires. These are available from 35-gauge (very fine but rare) to 18-gauge (thicker). Floristry tape is used in the construction of stems and bouquets. They contain a glue that is released when the tape is stretched. I use mainly nile green, brown and white tape from the Lion Brand tape company.

Tape shredder

This tool contains three razor blades to cut floristry tape into quarter-widths. I have a couple of tape shredders and have removed two blades from one of them so that it cuts the tape into half-widths. It is often best to use a tiny amount of cold cream rubbed onto the blades with a cotton bud and also a little onto the lid that presses against the blades – this will help the tape run smoothly against the blades as it can often stick to an excess of glue left behind from the tape. It is also wise to remove any excess build-up of glue from the blades using fine-nose pliers and also to replace the blades regularly. Handle with care at all times.

Paintbrushes and dusting brushes

Good-quality, synthetic brushes or synthetic-blend brushes from the art shop are best for flower-making. I use mainly short, flat, not too soft bristle brushes for applying layers of food colour dusts to flowers and leaves. It is best to keep brushes for certain colours so that it takes away the need to wash them quite so regularly. I use finer sable or synthetic-blend brushes for painting fine lines or detail spots onto petals.

Petal, flower and leaf cutters and veiners

There is a huge selection of petal, flower and leaf cutters available from cake decorating shops, both in metal and plastic. Petal and leaf moulds/veiners are made from food-grade silicone rubber. They are very useful for creating natural petal and leaf texturing for sugar work. The moulds have been made using mostly real plant material, giving the finished sugar flower a realistic finish. Like the flower cutters, there is an impressive selection of commercial veiners to choose from.

Posy picks

These are made from food-grade plastic and come in various sizes. They are used to hold the handle of a spray or bouquet of flowers into the cake. The food-grade plastic protects the cake of contamination from the wires and floristry tape used in the construction of floral sprays. Never push wires directly into a cake.

Stamens and thread

There is a huge selection of commercial stamens available from cake decorating shops. I use mainly fine white and seed-head stamens, which I can then colour using powder colours. Fine cotton thread is best for stamens. I use lace-making Brock 120 white thread, although some thicker threads may also be useful for larger

flowers. An emery board is great for fluffing up the tips of the thread to forms anthers.

Glue

Non-toxic glue sticks can be bought from stationery or art shops and are great for fixing ribbon to the cake drum's edge. Always make sure that the glue does not come into direct contact with the cake. I use

Homemade leaf/petal veiners

There are several craft products available that can be used to make moulds for leaves, petals, fruit, nuts, etc… It is important to try to find a food-grade product. Silicone plastique is a good medium to use with a quick-drying time. When making a mould of a petal or leaf it is important to choose items with prominent veins. Note that most flowers and foliage produce stronger veins as they age. To make a mould:

1 Silicone plastique can be purchased as a kit. Mix the two compounds together thoroughly. The white material is the base and the blue is the catalyst – once mixed you will have about 10 to 20 minutes' working time before the mixed medium sets – this often depends on the room temperature at the time. Flatten the product onto a sheet of plastic wrap or a plastic food bag: this is important as the product tends to stick to everything in its sight.

2 Press the back of your chosen leaf or petal into the silicone putty, taking care to press the surface evenly to avoid air bubbles, which will create a fault in the veiner. When the compound has set, simply peel off the leaf or petal. Trim away any excess silicone from around the mould using a pair of scissors.

3 Next, very lightly grease the leaf veiner with cold cream cleanser – be careful not to block up the veins with the cream as this will ruin the final result. Mix up another amount of the two compounds and press firmly on top of the first half of the leaf veiner, again taking care to press evenly. When the second half has set, pull the two sides apart: you now have a double-sided leaf veiner!

a hi-tack non-toxic craft glue to attach stamens to the end of wires. I feel that no harm is being done sticking inedible items together with other inedible items. However, the glue should not come into direct contact with the sugar petals as it will dissolve them.

Scissors, pliers and wire cutters

Fine embroidery and curved scissors are very useful for cutting fine petals, thread and ribbons too. Larger florist's scissors are useful for cutting wires and ribbon. Small, fine-nose pliers are another essential. Good-quality pliers from electrical supply shops are best – they are expensive but well worth the investment. Electrical wire cutters are useful for cutting heavier wires.

Plain-edge cutting wheel (PME) and scalpel

This is rather like a small double-sided pizza wheel. It is great for cutting out quick petals and leaves, and also for adding division lines to buds. A scalpel is essential for marking veins, adding texture and cutting out petal shapes too.

Tweezers

It is important to use fine, angled tweezers without ridges (or teeth). They are useful for pinching ridges on petals and holding very fine petals and stamens. They are also very handy when arranging flowers to push smaller items into difficult, tight areas of an arrangement or spray.

Metal ball tools (CC/Celcakes)

I use mostly metal ball tools to work the edges of petals and leaves. These are heavier than plastic ball tools, which means that less effort is needed to soften the paste. I mostly work the tool using a rubbing or rolling action against the paste, positioning it half on the petal/leaf edge and half on my hand or foam pad that the petal is resting against. It can also be used to 'cup' or hollow out petals to form interesting shapes.

Dresden/veining tool (J or PME)

The fine end of this tool is great for adding central veins to petals or leaves, and the broader end can be used for working the edges of a leaf to give a serrated effect or a 'double-frilled' effect on the edges of petals. Simply press the tool against the paste repeatedly to create a tight frilled effect or pull the tool against the paste on a non-stick board to create serrations. The fine end of the tool can also be used to cut into the edge of the paste to cut and flick finer serrated-edged leaves. I use a black tool by Jem for finer, smaller leaves and flowers, and the larger yellow PME tool for larger flowers.

Ceramic tools (HP/Holly Products)

A smooth ceramic tool is used for curling the edges of petals and hollowing out throats of small flowers, as well as serving the purpose of a mini rolling pin. Another of the ceramic tools, known as the silk veining tool, is wonderful for creating delicate veins and frills to petal edges.

Celsticks (CC/Celcakes)

Celsticks come in four sizes and are ideal for rolling out small petals and leaves and to create thick ridges. The pointed end of the tool is great for opening up the centre of 'hat'-type flowers. The rounded end can be used in the same way as a ball tool, to soften edges and hollow out petals.

Kitchen paper ring formers

These are great for holding and supporting petals to create a cupped shape as they dry allowing the paste/petal to breathe, which speeds up the drying process (plastic formers tend to slow down the drying process). To make, cut a strip of kitchen paper, twist it back onto itself and then tie it in a loop, or for larger petals, cut a sheet of kitchen paper diagonally across, twist and tie.

MATERIALS

Egg white

You will need fresh egg white to stick petals together and to sometimes alter the consistency of the paste if it is too dry. Many cake decorators avoid the use of fresh egg white because of salmonella scares. I continue to use Lion brand eggs and always work with a fresh egg white each time I make flowers. There are commercially available edible glues which can be used instead of egg white but I find that these tend to dissolve the sugar slightly before allowing it to dry, resulting in weak petals.

White vegetable fat

I use this to grease non-stick boards and then wipe of it off with dry kitchen paper. This does two things: it conditions the board, helping prevent the flowerpaste sticking to it, and it also removes excess food colour that might have been left from the previous flower-making session. You can also add a tiny amount of white fat to the paste if it is very sticky. However, you must not add too much as it will make the paste short and slow down the drying process. You must also be careful not to leave too much fat on the board as greasy patches will show up on the petals when you apply the dry dusting colours.

Cornflour bag

An essential if you have hot hands like mine! Cornflour is a lifesaver when the flowerpaste is sticky. It is best to make a cornflour bag using disposable nappy liners; these can be bought from most large chemists. Fold a couple of layers of nappy liners together and add a good tablespoon of cornflour on top. Tie the nappy liner together into a bag using ribbon or an elastic band. This bag is then used to lightly dust the paste prior to rolling it out and also on petals/leaves before they are placed into a veiner.

Petal dusts

These are my favourite forms of food colour. These food colour dusts contain a gum which helps them to adhere to the petal or leaf. They are wonderful for creating very soft and also very intense colouring to finished flowers. The dusts can be mixed together to form different colours or brushed on in layers which I find creates more interest and depth to the finished flower or leaf. White petal dust can be added to soften the colours (some cake decorators add cornflour but I find this weakens the gum content of the dust, often causing a streaky effect to the petal). If you are trying to create bold, strong colours it is best to dust the surface of the flowerpaste while it is still fairly pliable or at the leather-hard stage. A paint can also be made by adding clear alcohol (isopropyl) to the dust. This is good for adding spots and finer details. Another of my favourite uses of this dust is to add it to melted cocoa butter to make a paint that is ideal for painting designs onto the surface of a cake. Petal dusts can be used in small amounts to colour flowerpaste to create interesting and subtle base colours.

Paste food colours

I use only a small selection of paste food colours. I prefer to work with a white or a very pale base colour and then create stronger finished colours using powder food colours. I add paste colours into sugarpaste to cover the cakes but even then I am not a huge fan of strongly coloured cake coverings. It is best to mix up a small ball of sugarpaste with some paste food colour and then add this ball to the larger amount of paste – this will avoid you adding too much colour to the entire amount of sugarpaste. There's nothing worse than a screaming yellow cake!

Liquid colours

These are generally used to colour royal icing as they alter the consistency of flowerpaste, sugarpaste and almond paste but they can also be great to paint with. I use a small selection of liquid colours to paint fine spots and fine lines to petals. I mostly use cyclamen and poinsettia red liquid colours for flower-making.

Craft dusts

These are inedible and only intended for items that are not going to be eaten. Craft dusts are much stronger and much more light-fast than food colour dusts. Care must be taken as they do tend to migrate the moment you take the lid off the pot. Dust in an enclosed space as once these colours get into the air they have a habit of landing where you don't want them to. To prevent spotty cakes, it is best to keep the cake in a box while you are dusting the flowers, whether it is with these or petal dusts.

Edible glaze spray

There are several ways to glaze leaves. Recently I have been using an edible spray varnish made by Fabilo. This glaze can be used lightly for most leaves or sprayed in layers for shiny leaves and berries. Spray in a well-ventilated area, perhaps wearing a filter mask. Spraying leaves is much quicker than the method below which I also use from time to time.

Confectioner's varnish

Confectioner's varnish can be used neat to create a high glaze on berries and foliage. I mostly dilute the glaze with isopropyl alcohol (often sold as dipping solution or glaze cleaner in cake decorating shops). This lessens the shine, giving a more natural effect for most foliage and some petals. I mix the two liquids together in a clean jam jar with a lid. Do not shake as this produces air bubbles. Leaves can be dipped straight into the glaze, shaking off the excess before hanging to dry or placing onto kitchen paper to blot off any excess. The glaze can also be painted onto the leaf but I find the bristles of the brush pull off some of the dust colour, giving a streaky

effect. You need to watch the leaves as a build-up of glaze can give a streaky shiny finish which is not desirable. I use various strengths of glaze:

¾ glaze (1 part isopropyl alcohol to 3 parts confectioner's varnish) gives a high glaze but takes away the very plastic finish often left by full, undiluted confectioner's varnish.

½ glaze (equal proportions of the two). This is used to give a natural shine for many types of foliage, including ivy and rose leaves.

¼ glaze (3 parts isopropyl alcohol to 1 part confectioner's varnish). This is used for leaves and sometimes petals that don't require a shine but just need something stronger than just steaming to set the colour and remove the dusty finish.

When the varnish has dried, you might like to use a scalpel to scratch or etch through the glaze into the surface of the flowerpaste to create fine white veins on the likes of ivy leaves.

RECIPES

Here are the recipes that will help you along your way with the projects in this book.
There are recipes for modelling pastes, royal icing and two wonderful fruitcakes too.

FRUITCAKE

Double the quantities for a three-tier wedding cake and line another small tin just in case there is some cake mixture left over. This recipe will fill a 30 cm (12 in) round cake tin, plus a little extra for a smaller cake. Even if I only need a 20 cm (8 in) oval cake I still make up this full quantity and bake extra cakes with the remaining mixture – it is hardly worth turning the oven on just for one small cake. The variety and amount of each dried fruit can be changed to suit your own taste.

INGREDIENTS

1 kg (2 lb 3 oz/8 cups) raisins
1 kg (2 lb 3 oz/8 cups) sultanas
500 g (1 lb 2 oz/4 cups) dried figs, chopped
500 g (1 lb 2 oz/4 cups) prunes, chopped
250 g (9 oz/2 cups) natural colour glacé cherries, halved
125 g (4½ oz/1 cup) dried apricots, chopped
125 g (4½ oz/1 cup) dried or glacé pineapple, chopped
Grated zest and juice of 1 orange
200 ml (7 fl oz/½ cup) brandy (the odd dash of Cointreau or cherry brandy can be good too)
500 g (1 lb 2 oz/2 cups) unsalted butter, at room temperature
250 g (9 oz/2 cups) light muscovado sugar
250 g (9 oz/2 cups) dark muscovado sugar
4 tsp apricot jam
8 tsp golden syrup
1 tsp each of ground ginger, allspice, nutmeg, cloves and cinnamon
½ tsp mace
500 g (1 lb 2 oz/4 cups) plain flour
250 g (9 oz/1½ cups) ground almonds
10 large free-range eggs, at room temperature

1 Use a large pair of scissors to halve and chop the various fruit that require it from the list. Add or subtract the fruit accordingly to suit your taste, but make sure the weight remains the same. Mix the dried fruit, orange zest and juice, and alcohol together in a plastic container with a lid. Seal the container and leave to soak for about a week if time allows. Otherwise overnight will do.

2 Preheat the oven to 140°C/275°F (gas 1). Cream the butter in a large bowl until soft. Gradually add the two types of sugar and beat the together. Stir in the apricot jam, golden syrup and spices (including the mace).

3 Sieve the flour into a separate bowl and stir in the almonds.

4 Beat the eggs together and add slowly to the butter/sugar mixture, alternating it with the flour/almond mix. Do not add the eggs too quickly as the mixture might curdle.

5 Before you add the fruit, set aside a small amount of un-fruited batter – this will be used on top of the fruited batter to stop the fruit catching on the top in the oven. Mix the soaked fruit into the remaining larger amount of batter. Grease and line the tin(s) with non-stick parchment paper. Fill the tin with batter to the required depth – I usually aim for about two-thirds the depth of the tin. Apply a thin layer of the un-fruited batter on top and smooth over. Bake for 4 to 6 hours, depending on the size of the cake. It is important to smell when the cake is ready – some ovens cook faster than others. The cake should shrink slightly from the sides of the tin, be firm to the touch and smell wonderful. If in doubt test with a skewer – if it comes out clean the cake is ready.

6 Allow the cake to cool slightly in the tin, add a couple of extra dashes of alcohol, and leave to cool further in the tin. Store wrapped in non-stick parchment paper and plastic wrap. Allow to mature for as long as you have – a few days to a few months works well.

SUNSHINE FRUITCAKE

This is a wonderful option for those who prefer a lighter cake. The white chocolate gives a very pleasant aftertaste.

INGREDIENTS

150 g (5½ oz/1¼ cups) glacé cherries (multi-coloured ones look great), halved, washed and allowed to dry

100 g (3½ oz/1 cup) ground almonds

100 g (3½ oz/½ cup) each of dried ready-to-eat pineapple, mango, peach, apricot and pear

1 medium Bramley apple, grated

50 g (2 oz/2 squares) grated white chocolate

75 g (2½ oz/¾ cup) dried cranberries

3 Tbsp brandy (cherry brandy or Calvados work well too!) (optional)

225 g (8 oz/1 cup) unsalted butter, at room temperature

225 g (8 oz/1 cup) caster sugar

1 tsp salt

4 large free-range eggs

250 g (9 oz/2 cups) plain flour mixed with ¼ level tsp baking powder

1 tsp vanilla essence

1 Preheat the oven to 180°C/350°F (gas 4). Line a 20 cm (8 in) round cake tin with greaseproof paper.

2 Toss the glacé cherries in the ground almonds and set aside. Chop the remaining exotic fruits and then toss them with the grated apple and white chocolate, dried cranberries and brandy. Leave for an hour or so.

3 In a separate bowl, beat the butter, sugar and salt together until pale and fluffy. Beat in the eggs, one at a time, alternating with a tablespoon of flour and beating well between each addition. Add and stir in the remaining flour and vanilla essence. Then add the exotic fruit mixture and the cherries with the ground almonds and stir well to incorporate the fruit.

4 Spoon the mixture into the prepared cake tin. Level the top and bake at 180°C/350°F (gas 4) for the first 30 minutes, turning the heat down to 150°C/300°F (gas 3) for the remaining cooking time (2 to 2½ hours total baking time). Cover the cake with foil if you feel the cake is catching or turn the oven down a little. Leave the cake to cool in the tin before turning out.

ROYAL ICING

This recipe is ideal for small amounts of royal icing required to create brush embroidery, lace, embroidery and other piped techniques.

INGREDIENTS

1 medium free-range egg white, at room temperature

225 g (8 oz/1¾ cups) icing sugar, sifted

1 Wash the mixer bowl and the beater with a concentrated detergent and then scald with boiling water to remove any traces of grease and leftover detergent. Dry thoroughly.

2 Place the egg white into the mixer bowl and the majority of the icing sugar and mix the two together with a metal spoon.

3 Fix the bowl and beater to the machine and beat on the lowest speed until the icing has reached full peak – this takes about 8 minutes. You may need to add a little extra sugar if the mixture is too soft.

COLD PORCELAIN

This is an inedible air-drying craft paste that can be used in almost exactly the same way as flowerpaste. The bonus with this paste is that the flowers made from it are much stronger and less prone to breakages. However, because it is inedible, anything made from this paste cannot come into direct contact with a cake's surface, so flowers made from cold porcelain need to be placed in a vase, container, candle-holder or Perspex plaque. I tend to treat flowers made with this paste pretty much as I would fresh or silk flowers. There are several commercial cold porcelain pastes available but you can make your own – the recipe below is the one that I prefer. I use measuring spoons and measuring cups to measure out the ingredients.

INGREDIENTS

2½ Tbsp baby oil

115 ml (4 fl oz/½ cup) non-toxic hi-tack craft glue (Impex)

115 ml (4 fl oz/½ cup) white PVA wood glue (Liberon Super wood glue or Elmers)

125 g (4½ oz/1 cup) cornflour

Permanent white artist's gouache paint

1 Work in a well-ventilated area when making this paste. Wear a filter mask if you suffer from asthma. Measure the baby oil and the two glues together in a non-stick saucepan to form an emulsion. Stir the cornflour into the mixture. It will go lumpy at this stage but this is normal!

2 Place the pan over a medium heat and stir the paste with a heavy-duty plastic or wooden spoon. The paste will gradually come away from the base and sides of the pan to form a ball around the spoon. Scrape any uncooked paste from

the spoon and add it to the mix. The cooking time will vary – usually around 10 minutes – between gas, electric and ceramic hobs, but the general rule is the lower the heat and the slower you mix the paste, the smoother the resulting paste will be. I'm impatient so I tend to turn up the heat a little to cook faster. Keep on stirring the paste to cook it evenly. You will need to split the paste and press the inner parts of the ball against the heat of the pan to cook it too – be careful not to overcook.

3 Turn the paste onto a non-stick board and knead until smooth. The paste is quite hot at this stage. The kneading should help distribute some heat through the paste to cook any undercooked areas. If the paste is very sticky then you will need to put it back in the pan to cook longer. It is better if it is slightly undercooked as you can always add heat later – if the paste is overcooked then it is almost impossible to work with.

4 Wrap in plastic wrap and leave to cool – moisture will build up on the surface of the paste that, if left, will encourage mould growth, so it is important to re-knead the paste when cool and then re-wrap. Place in a plastic food bag and then in an airtight container, and store at room temperature. This paste has been known to work well two years after it was made if stored like this.

5 Prior to making flowers you will need to add a smidge of permanent white gouache paint. The paste looks white but by its very nature dries clear, giving a translucence to the finished flower. Adding the paint makes the finish

more opaque. Handling the paste is quite similar to working with sugar except I use cold cream cleanser instead of white vegetable fat, and glue or anti-bacterial wipes/water to moisten the petals to stick them. Cornflour is used as for handling flowerpaste. The paste shrinks a little as it dries – this is because of the glue. This can be disconcerting to begin with but you will gradually get used to it and it can be an advantage when making miniature flowers.

FLOWERPASTE

I always buy ready-made commercial flowerpaste (APOC) as it tends to be more consistent than homemade pastes. The following recipe is the one I used prior to discovering the joys of ready-made flowerpaste! Gum tragacanth gives the paste stretch and strength too.

INGREDIENTS

5 tsp cold water
2 tsp powdered gelatine
500 g (1 lb 2 oz/3 cups) icing sugar, sifted
3 tsp gum tragacanth
2 tsp liquid glucose
3 tsp white vegetable fat, plus 1 extra tsp to add later
1 large fresh egg white

1 Mix the cold water and gelatine together in a small bowl and leave to stand for 30 minutes. Sift the icing sugar and gum tragacanth together into the bowl of a heavy-duty mixer and fit to the machine.

2 Place the bowl with the gelatine mixture over a saucepan of hot water and stir until the gelatine has dissolved.

Warm a teaspoon in hot water and then measure out the liquid glucose – the heat of the spoon should help to ease the glucose on its way. Add the glucose and 3 teaspoons of white fat to the gelatine mixture, and continue to heat until all the ingredients have dissolved and are thoroughly mixed together.

3 Add the dissolved gelatine mixture to the icing sugar/gum tragacanth with the egg white. Beat at the mixer's lowest speed, then gradually increase the speed to maximum until the paste is white and stringy.

4 Remove the paste from the bowl, knead into a smooth ball and cover with the remaining teaspoon of white fat – this helps to prevent the paste forming a dry crust that can leave hard bits in the paste at the rolling out stage. Place in a plastic food bag and store in an airtight container. Allow the paste to rest and mature for 12 hours before use.

5 The paste should be well-kneaded before you start to roll it out or model it into a flower shape, otherwise it has a tendency to dry out and crack around the edges. This is an air-drying paste so when you are not using it make sure it is well wrapped in a plastic bag. If you have cut out lots of petals, cover them over with a plastic bag.

TECHNIQUES

These are some of the essential techniques that you will use time and time again when creating floral celebration cakes.

COATING A CAKE WITH ALMOND PASTE

I adore the flavour and texture of almond paste. A layer of natural-coloured white almond paste gives a smooth, round-edged base on which to apply a layer of sugarpaste, creating a more professional finish and excellent eating quality too! It is important that the work surface is free of flour or cornflour, as if any gets trapped between the almond paste and the sugarpaste it can cause fermentation, encouraging air bubbles. It is best, but not always essential, to leave the almond paste-coated cake to dry out and firm up for a few days prior to icing.

1 Before applying any form of coating, the cake must be level. To do this, carefully cut off the top of the cake if it has formed a dome during baking. Then turn the cake upside down so that the flat bottom becomes the top. Fill any large indentations with almond paste if required. Place the cake onto a thin cake board the same size as the cake so that it is easier to move. You might also prefer to add a strip of almond paste around the base of the cake to seal it and the cake board tightly together.

2 Warm some apricot jam and a dash of water, brandy or Cointreau, and then sieve to make an apricot glaze that can be painted onto the surface of the cake. This will help to stick the almond paste to the cake and help seal it to keep it fresh. Apricot glaze is used as the colour is not too dark and the flavour tends not to fight with the taste of the cake or almond paste. You may also be able to buy ready-sieved apricot glaze in a jar – which also benefits from a dash of alcohol.

3 You will need a long, non-stick rolling pin large enough to roll out almond paste to cover at least a 30 cm (12 in) cake. Plastic smoothers are also essential to create a professional finish: a curved smoother for the top of the cake and a square-edged one for the sides. Rolling out almond paste to an even thickness can be tricky, and a novice cake decorator might find a pair of marzipan spacers useful to roll against. Depending which way they are placed, they can produce thick or thin sheets of almond paste/sugarpaste. It is best to store the paste in a warm place prior to kneading to help soften it slightly – otherwise it can be quite hard to work with. Knead the paste on a clean, dry surface to make it pliable.

4 Lightly dust the work surface with icing sugar. Place the almond paste on top and if needed position the spacers on either side of the paste. Roll the paste out lengthways using the non-stick rolling pin. Turn it sideways and reposition the spacers on either side again. Continue to roll out the paste until it is large enough to cover the cake. A measuring tape, string or even using the length of the rolling pin to gauge the exact size of the cake top and its sides can be useful. It is always best to allow slightly more than you think you will need, especially for awkward-shaped cakes or anything with corners to it.

5 Using a round-edged plastic smoother, polish and smooth out the surface of the almond paste. Start gently, gradually increasing the pressure to even out any slightly uneven areas of the paste.

6 Place the rolling pin on top of the almond paste and use it to help lift the paste over the cake. Remove the rolling pin and ease the almond paste into place. Smooth the surface of the cake to exclude any air bubbles. Tuck the paste to fit the sides. If you are working on a cake with corners, then concentrate on these first of all.

7 Use the curved-edge smoother to polish the top of the cake. Use strong, firm hand movements to 'iron out' any imperfections. Use the edge of the straight-edged smoother to cut and flick away the excess paste from the base of the cake. Finally, use the straight-edged smoother to iron out the sides of the cake using a fair amount of pressure. Place the cake onto a sheet of greaseproof paper and, if time allows, leave to firm up overnight or for a few days prior to coating with sugarpaste.

COATING A CAKE AND CAKE DRUM WITH SUGARPASTE

Plastic sugarpaste smoothers are essential when covering a cake with sugarpaste. The round-edged smoother is good for working on the top of the cake and the straight-edged smoother is good for working on the sides, giving a sharper edge at the base. Covering a cake with sugarpaste is a fairly straightforward process – however, practice is needed to achieve very neat results. If you are colouring the sugarpaste it is best to use paste food colour or to thicken liquid colours with icing sugar. It is safer to colour a small amount of sugarpaste and then knead this into the larger amount of paste to control the depth of colour rather than create a paste that is too brightly coloured.

1 Knead the sugarpaste on a clean, dry sugar- and flour-free surface until smooth and pliable. Take care not to knead in too many air bubbles. When fully kneaded, lightly dust the work surface with sieved icing sugar and place the sugarpaste on top, with any cracks against the work surface. Roll out, smooth and polish the paste as described for the almond paste coating.

2 Moisten the surface of the almond paste with clear alcohol (Cointreau, kirsch or white rum can all be used). Use a sponge to apply the alcohol as this gives a more even covering. Any dry areas will encourage air bubbles to be trapped between the almond paste and the sugarpaste. The alcohol helps to stick the sugarpaste to the almond paste and also acts as an antibacterial agent.

3 Pick up the sugarpaste onto the rolling pin and lower it over the cake, taking care to position the paste so that it will cover the sides evenly. Remove the rolling pin. Use your hands and then the round-edged smoother to create a smooth finish and eliminate air bubbles. Next, lift and ease the paste against the sides of the cake. If the cake has corners or points, deal with these first as they often crack or tear. Be careful not to stretch the sugarpaste too much as you work. Trim the excess paste from the base of the cake using a flat knife or the edge of a straight-edged smoother. Use the same smoother to iron out the sides of the cake. Use a pin to prick any air bubbles/pockets that might appear (brightly coloured glass head pins are best for this job so that you can easily spot them when not in use) and then smooth over with the sugarpaste smoothers. Continue to use the curved-edge smoother on the top of the cake and the straight-edged smoother on the sides to create a good, even finish. The edges of the coating or any difficult points or curved areas can be given extra attention with a pad of sugarpaste pressed into your palm and used to polish the paste.

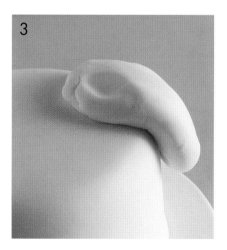

4 To coat a cake drum, roll out the sugarpaste and carefully place it over a drum moistened with clear alcohol. Smooth over with the round-edged smoother and then trim off the excess with a flat knife. Smooth the cut edge with a smoother to neaten it. Next, polish with a pad of sugarpaste pressed into your palm.

5 Soften a small amount of sugarpaste with clear alcohol (Cointreau, kirsch or white rum) and place at the centre of the cake drum. Carefully lower the cake which should be on a cake board of the same size over the top. Gently press down the top of the cake with the round-edged smoother to bond the cake and the drum together. Use the straight-edged smoother to blend and create a good join between the cake and the drum. Smooth over any areas that need extra attention with the sugarpaste pad technique.

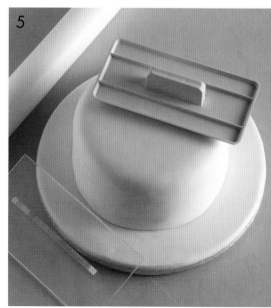

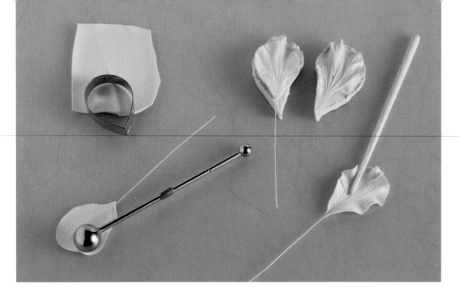

WIRING PETALS AND LEAVES

This is my favourite method of constructing flowers. It gives the flowers much more movement and extra strength too, resulting in fewer breakages.

1 Knead a piece of flowerpaste and form roughly into the shape of the petal or leaf you are making. Press it down against a non-stick board to flatten it slightly. Use a celstick or rolling pin to roll the flowerpaste, leaving a ridge for the wire. Try to create a tapered ridge, angling the pin slightly so that the ridge is thicker at the base of the petal/leaf. The thickness and length of the ridge will depend on the size of the petal/ leaf you are making. There are also boards available commercially which have grooves in them that create a similar ridged effect when the paste is rolled over them. These can be great for smaller petals and leaves but I find they produce too fine a ridge for many of the larger flowers that I make.

2 Cut out the petal/leaf shape using a cutter, scalpel or plain-edge cutting wheel, leaving the ridge to run down the centre. If you are using a cutter, lift up the shape and place it onto a very light dusting of cornflour and then press firmly with the cutter and scrub it slightly against the paste and the board so that the shape remains slightly stuck in the cutter. This will enable

you to quickly rub the edge of the cutter to create a cleaner-cut edge, removing any fuzzy bits!

3 Moisten the wire very slightly – too much will result in the paper coming off the wire and also slow down the drying process of the petal on the wire. Hold the ridge firmly between your finger and thumb, and hold the wire in the other hand very close to the end of the wire that is being inserted into the shape. Push the wire in gradually so that it supports a third to half the length. Use a ball tool to soften and thin the edge of the shape using a rolling action, working the tool half on your hand/foam pad and half on the edge of the paste.

4 Place the petal/leaf into a double-sided petal/leaf veiner and press the two sides firmly against the shape to texture it.

5 A frilled edge can be added using a cocktail stick or a ceramic veining tool, working at intervals to encourage a natural frilled effect.

GLAZING

Glazing can help give a leaf or petal a more realistic appearance. Care must be taken not to glaze flowers too heavily as this can make them look unnatural.

STEAMING

Using powder colours on sugar flowers often leaves a slightly dry-looking finished flower; this can be changed to create a slightly more waxy appearance and also help to set the colour to stop it leaving marks on the surface of the coated cake. Hold each flower in the steam from a boiling kettle for a few seconds, or until the surface turns slightly shiny. Take care not to scald yourself and also not to get the sugar too wet as it will dissolve fairly fast. Allow the flower to dry before wiring into a spray. If you are trying to create a velvety finish to something like a red rose, then the steaming process can be used and then re-dust the flower – you will find that this will hold onto more dust, giving the desired effect.

EDIBLE GOLD AND SILVER LEAF

I love using sheets of gold 23-carat and silver leaf to embellish side designs on cakes. However, the sheets are very fine and tend to tear and fly very easily. Using the following method creates a more convenient way to control this delightful trickster!

1 Roll out some well-kneaded flowerpaste very thinly using a non-stick rolling pin. Lift up the paste and place the sticky side that was against the non-stick board carefully over a whole single sheet of gold/silver leaf. Smooth the flowerpaste from behind onto the leaf to adhere the two together. Turn the flowerpaste over to reveal the coated side. Trim off the excess uncoated paste from the edges. Leave to set for about 20 minutes to give a more paper-like finish and then cut out shapes using a paper punch or flower/leaf cutters. Keep any leftover pieces of the gilded paste to use at a later stage – these dried pieces of paste can be broken into small shards and used to create an alternative decorative effect combined with painted images, added to piped embroidery designs or even combined with dragées.

2 A crackle effect can also be achieved by resting the gold/silver leaf-coated flowerpaste a little and then re-rolling to reveal the colour of the flowerpaste beneath – this can be particularly effective using purple, red or black flowerpaste as a backing for gold or silver leaf.

3 For a jewelled, textured effect, sprinkle some coloured sugar crystal sprinkles on top of the freshly bonded gold/silver leaf flowerpaste and then quickly roll this into the surface using a non-stick rolling pin to embed the crystals into the paste.

FLOWERS, FRUIT AND NUTS

Fringed nigella

I came across this unusual fringed form of nigella recently – it was quite a surprise as nigella, or 'love in a mist' as it is often called, is generally a much smaller delicate blue flower! There are some green versions of this flower too.

STAMEN CENTRE

1 Cut several short lengths of 33-gauge white wire. Blend a small ball of pale green cold porcelain onto the end to create a fine, tapered carrot shape. This is to represent each section of the ovary at the centre of the flower. Pinch a slight ridge down one side at the base. Repeat to make 5 to 8 sections. As the cold porcelain begins to firm up you should be able to curl and twist each section prior to taping together with quarter-width nile green floristry tape. I use cold porcelain for the centre as it enables the stamens to be glued easily around it to create a neat join.

2 Dust the centre with vine green petal dust. Next, take small sets of white seed-head stamens (3 to 5 in a set) and glue each set together at the centre with non-toxic craft glue. Flatten and work the glue from the centre towards either end of the stamens. Repeat with the other groups, trying not to apply too much glue as this will cause bulk and also take much longer to dry. Once the glue has set, cut the stamens in half and then trim away the excess using sharp scissors to leave only a short length to each group with a fine line of glue holding them together.

3 Apply a little more glue to the base of each short stamen group and attach around the base of the ovary sections. Squeeze the base of the stamens into place. Leave to set. Dust the filaments (the length) with vine petal dust and the tips with a mixture of daffodil and sunflower.

FRINGED PETALS

4 These vary in size and are a little random in their make-up too which is good for the flower-maker! Cut several lengths of 33-, 30- or 28-gauge white wire, depending on the size of petal you are working on. Blend a ball of well-kneaded white flowerpaste onto the wire to create a long, tapered petal shape. Keep the base broad and the tip fine. Flatten the shape against the non-stick board using the flat side of the stargazer B petal veiner. You might need to trim the edges slightly to neaten them up with fine scissors or a plain-edge cutting wheel.

5 Soften the edge of the petal with the ball tool and then texture using the double-sided stargazer B petal veiner.

6 Use fine curved scissors to make a long cut on either edge of the petal to create a tri-lobed shaped petal. Open up the sections and then add finer shorter snips to the edges of the three sections.

7 Next, place the petal against the non-stick board and press each of the fringed sections with the broad end of the Dresden tool to thin them out slightly.

8 Pinch the petal from the base to the tip to create a central vein. Repeat to make numerous petals, curving them slightly to give the flower more movement.

COLOURING AND ASSEMBLY

9 The petals can be dusted before or after assembly with a mixture of plum, coral and white petal dusts, concentrating most of the colour at the base of each petal. Tinge the edges with vine green and small amounts of foliage green too. Tape the petals around the centre using quarter-width nile green floristry tape.

LEAVES

10 These are very fine and look good made from fine 33-gauge white wires and twisted nile green floristry tape. Add groups of leaves directly behind the flower. Dust them with foliage and vine green.

Sweet violet

The sweet violet, with its heady fragrance, has been used to symbolise love for thousands of years. It is also the flower of Aphrodite, the goddess of love. In years gone by, violets were strewn on the floors of cottages and churches to conceal the musty smell of damp and to sweeten the air. Although there are cutters available for making violets, I actually prefer to use the method that was first taught to me 20-odd years ago: simply using a pair of scissors to cut the varying sizes of petal and then pinching and pulling each petal between finger and thumb to create the desired petal shape. This method, commonly known as the pulled flower method, can be used to make many types of filler flowers.

MATERIALS

White and holly/ivy flowerpaste
Cornflour bag (p 11)
26-gauge white wire
Nile green floristry tape
Fresh egg white
African violet, deep purple, daffodil, white, sunflower, vine green, foliage and aubergine petal dusts
Black paste food colour
Isopropyl alcohol
Edible spray varnish

EQUIPMENT

Smooth ceramic tool
Scissors
Fine-nose pliers
Non-stick rolling pin
Heart-shaped cutters
Dresden tool
Ball tool
Violet leaf veiner (SKGI)
Dimpled foam
Dusting brushes
Fine paintbrush
Calyx cutter (R15 OP) (optional)

FLOWERS

1 Form a ball of well-kneaded white flowerpaste into a cone shape. Open up and thin out the broad end using the pointed end of the smooth ceramic tool – you might need a light dusting of cornflour to prevent the paste sticking to the tool.

2 Next, divide the shape into five unequal-sized petals using a pair of scissors. You are aiming to end up with one larger lip petal with two small petals on either side of it, plus two medium-sized petals together at the top of the flower.

3 Spread the petals apart and then carefully pinch each into a pointed shape between your finger and thumb. The next stage is to 'pull' each petal between your finger and thumb: hold the petal firmly across the top with your thumb uppermost and your forefinger supporting the underside of the petal. Rub your finger against the petal but keep your thumb steady. This will flatten the petal and enlarge it. Repeat the process on all the petals.

4 Rest the flower over your forefinger and gently broaden and thin each petal using the ceramic tool.

5 Pinch the underside of the large petal to create a central vein and a curve to the petal. Pull and curl the two small side petals down towards the large petal and curl the two medium petals backwards. Correct the back of the flower into a fine pointed shape.

LEAVES

7 Roll out some holly/ivy flowerpaste, leaving a thick ridge for the wire. Cut out the leaf shape using a heart-shaped cutter. Insert a wire moistened with fresh egg white into about half the length of the thick ridge. The gauge will depend on the size of the leaf.

8 Use the Dresden tool to pull out serrations on the edge of the leaf at intervals. Soften the edge with the ball tool and then texture using the violet leaf veiner. Pinch the leaf from behind to accentuate the central vein and give an angle at the indent of the heart shape. Allow to firm up on dimpled foam for a little while before dusting.

10 Use a fine paintbrush and black paste food colour diluted with isopropyl alcohol to paint a series of fine lines on the base petal.

11 Curve the stem of the flower using fine-nose pliers. Add a couple of fine pointed floristry tape bracts part way down the stem. Add a calyx if required – here I have simply dusted a mixture of vine green and foliage petal dusts where the stem joins the back of the flower.

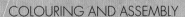

6 Tape over a 26-gauge white wire with quarter-width nile green floristry tape. Bend a hook in the end using fine-nose pliers, moisten with fresh egg white and then pull the wire through the centre and out behind the two medium petals. Try to embed the hook into the thickness around the centre to secure and support the shape. Add a stamen if desired. Allow to firm up a little before colouring.

COLOURING AND ASSEMBLY

9 Dust the flower with African violet petal dust. Leave a pale white area at the centre of the broad petal. Define the edge with a little deep purple. Add a yellow highlight in the broad petal with a mixture of daffodil and white petal dusts. Add a tiny amount of sunflower petal dust at the very centre of the flower using a fine paint-brush.

12 Dust the leaves with foliage and vine green petal dusts. Add the odd tinge of aubergine. Spray lightly with edible spray varnish.

Hearts entangled

Here is one of my favourite succulents – often known as hearts entangled or string of hearts (*Ceropegia woodii*). The variety used here has patterned leaves but other varieties have plain green leaves too if you are feeling a bit lazy! I have created only the foliage – the curious tiny flowers are like parachutes that trap insects, encouraging pollination.

LEAVES

1 The leaves could be made with small heart cutters – however, I find this makes them look a little mass-produced and so I prefer to make them using a pulled/freehand method. Cut lots of short lengths of 33- or 30-gauge white wire, depending on the size of leaf you are making. If you can buy 36- or 35-gauge wire, then that is even better for the smallest leaves.

2 Take a small ball of well-kneaded pale green flowerpaste and form it into a cone shape. Insert a wire moistened with fresh egg white into the broad end of the cone and then place against the non-stick board. Use your fingers to press and squeeze the flowerpaste against the board to form a very naïve heat shape. If you are worried about leaving your fingerprints, then you might prefer to place a plastic food bag over the top prior to forming the shape.

3 Next, hollow out the underside of the leaf using the small ball tool, working on both sides to encourage more of a heart shape. Pinch the leaf from behind to create a very gentle central vein. Repeat to make lots of leaves, pairing them as you work.

ASSEMBLY AND COLOURING

4 I prefer to tape the leaves onto a long stem prior to colouring but you might prefer to work the other way. Tape two tiny leaves onto the end of a 28-gauge white wire using quarter-width nile green floristry tape. Continue to add the leaves in pairs down the stem, gradually increasing in size as you work. Add extra wire if needed to support the length.

5 Dust the back of each leaf with a mixture of plum and aubergine petal dusts. Catch the upper edges here and there too, and also the trailing stems benefit from a light dusting. Use a mixture of foliage and white to dust the upper surface of the leaves. Dilute some foliage with isopropyl alcohol and paint darker green splodges onto the surface of each leaf. Leave to dry and then add some diluted spots of white bridal satin too. Spray with edible spray varnish or steam to set the colour, trying not to make the leaves too shiny.

MATERIALS

33-, 30- and 28-gauge white wires
Pale green flowerpaste
Fresh egg white
Plastic food bag
Nile green floristry tape
Plum, aubergine, foliage, white and white bridal satin petal dusts
Isopropyl alcohol
Edible spray varnish

EQUIPMENT

Wire cutters
Non-stick board
Small ball tool
Dusting brushes
Fine paintbrush

Japanese painted fern

I first came across these Japanese ferns (*Athyrium niponicum*) with painted faces in a seed/plant catalogue. Several of these unusual ferns were pictured but it was this purple-tinged variety that grabbed my attention the most. I love using foliage, and these decorative, colourful forms are ideal for adding interest to sprays and arrangements.

1 Make sure the very pale green flowerpaste is very well kneaded. Using the celstick, roll out the paste onto a fine grooved board or roll the paste leaving a fine ridge for the wire. The paste needs to be rolled very fine to allow you to retrieve it easily from the fern cutters. Cut out the fern sections using the three sizes of Australian fern cutters; beware the smallest cutter can be very tricky! The leaves grow almost in pairs of the same size down the stem. Insert a 33- or 30-gauge white wire into each leaf, depending on the size of the leaf. Alternatively, roll out the flowerpaste thinly, cut out the leaves and attach the wire covered with a thin layer of paste to patch onto the back.

2 Work the edges of each leaf using the broad end of the Dresden tool to create an almost feathered effect. Pinch a central vein from the base to the tip. Curve slightly. Repeat to make lots of leaves.

COLOURING AND ASSEMBLY

3 Dust from the edges of each leaf with a mixture of African violet and plum petal dusts. Use a light dusting of moss and foliage and a touch of white bridal satin on the front of the leaves – try not to let the green dominate the foliage. Dilute some plum petal dust with isopropyl alcohol and paint fine veins onto the front and back of each leaf, concentrating mainly on the central vein.

4 Tape the leaves onto a 26-gauge white wire using quarter-width nile green floristry tape, starting with a medium-size leaf at the very end followed by the smallest leaves in pairs down the stem and then gradually working through the other sizes to create the required length of fern. Introduce a 22-gauge white wire to the stem if a very large length is required. Dust the main stem with plum, African violet and a light dusting of aubergine too. Spray very lightly with edible spray varnish or steam to set the colour.

MATERIALS

Very pale green flowerpaste
33-, 30-, 26- and 22-gauge white wires
African violet, plum, moss, foliage, white bridal satin and aubergine petal dusts
Isopropyl alcohol
Nile green floristry tape
Edible spray varnish

EQUIPMENT

Celstick
Fine grooved board
Australian fern cutter set (APOC)
Dresden tool
Dusting brushes
Fine paintbrush

Blue sun orchid

It can be quite difficult finding attractive blue flowers to use on cakes. This version of the blue sun orchid was designed and made by my friend Sathya. I needed a blue flower for a man's cake so she kindly donated this species!

MATERIALS
30- and 28-gauge white wires
White flowerpaste
Fresh egg white
Nile green floristry tape
African violet, deep purple, plum, white, daffodil, sunflower and vine petal dusts
Isopropyl alcohol

EQUIPMENT
Ceramic tool (HP)
Fine scissors
Non-stick rolling pin
Spathoglottis orchid cutter set (TT825-826)
Cupped Christmas rose petal veiner (SKGI)
Dresden tool
Dusting brushes
Fine paintbrush

COLUMN

1 Insert a 30-gauge white wire into a small ball of white flowerpaste. Thin down the base of the ball to create a slender teardrop shape. Hollow out the underside of the column using the rounded end of the ceramic tool. Texture the top tip of the column by snipping it with fine scissors. Indent at the centre using the pointed end of the ceramic tool. Curve slightly.

OUTER PETALS AND SEPALS

2 All five outer petals are made in the same way with the same size cutter. Roll out some white flowerpaste thinly, leaving a thick ridge for the wire. Cut out the petal shape using the larger cutter from the spathoglottis orchid set.

3 Insert a 28-gauge white wire moistened with fresh egg white into the thick ridge to support about half the length. Soften the edge and then vein using the cupped Christmas rose petal veiner.

4 Pinch the base of the petal through to the tip to create a central vein, then curve backwards. Repeat to make six petals/sepals.

ASSEMBLY AND COLOURING

5 Using quarter-width nile green floristry tape, tape one petal underneath the column to represent the lip and then two at the side to represent the wing petals. Add the remaining three petals evenly spaced behind them to represent the dorsal and lateral sepals.

6 Work a ball of white flowerpaste behind the petals to cover about 2.5 cm (1 in) of the wire to create a fleshier feel to the back of the flower. Work the paste into the base of the petals using the broad end of the Dresden tool.

7 Dust the flower with a mixture of African violet, deep purple, plum and white petal dusts. Add stronger colouring to the edges of each petal. Dust the centre of the textured section on the column with a mixture of daffodil and sunflower petal dusts. Dust the neck of the flower with vine green petal dust.

8 Dilute some African violet and deep purple petal dusts with isopropyl alcohol and paint some fine spotted detail to the lip and wing petals.

Pachyveria succulent

These cultivated fleshy succulents are a cross hybridisation between *Pachyphytum* and *Echeveria*. Succulents are great to make as no cutters or veiners are required and there is a good excuse for working the paste on the thicker side too!

MATERIALS

Pale holly/ivy flowerpaste

33-, 30-, 28-, 26-gauge white wires

Fresh egg white

White floristry tape

Forest, foliage, edelweiss, plum and aubergine petal dusts

Edible spray varnish

EQUIPMENT

Medium metal ball tool (CC)

Dusting brushes

1 Roll a ball of pale holly/ivy flowerpaste. Form it into a teardrop shape and insert a wire moistened with fresh egg white – the gauge will depend on the size of leaf you are making. Work the paste at the base of the cone down onto the wire to form a 'neck'. Flatten the shape a little, leaving a thicker area at the centre.

2 Hollow the whole leaf slightly using the medium metal ball tool. The pressure of the tool against the wire will create a central vein. Pinch the tip into a sharp point. Repeat to make numerous leaves in varying sizes.

3 Tape the leaves together to form a rosette shape using quarter-width white floristry tape, starting with the smallest leaves snuggled tightly together. Gradually increase the size of the leaves as you work and use half-width white floristry tape for the larger leaves.

4 Dust the rosette leaves and stem as a whole using a mixture of forest, foliage and edelweiss. Tinge the tips and edges as desired – I tend to use a mixture of plum and aubergine petal dusts. Glaze lightly with edible spray varnish or steam gently to remove the dusted finish.

Dianthus

Often known as Pinks, there are about 300 species of dianthus from Europe, Asia, Africa and North America. The single dianthus illustrated here is quite simple to make and is a very pretty filler flower; it also works well in bunches on its own.

MATERIALS

White seed-head stamens
Hi-tack non-toxic craft glue
33-, 28- and 26-gauge white wires
Pale pink and pale holly/ivy flowerpaste
Fresh egg white
Plum, white, foliage and aubergine petal dusts
Cyclamen liquid food colour
Clear alcohol (Cointreau or kirsch)
Nile green floristry tape

EQUIPMENT

Fine scissors
Non-stick board
Celstick
Dianthus cutter (TT459)
Dresden tool
Fine calyx cutter (optional)
Leaf/petal veiner
Plain-edge cutting wheel
Dusting brushes
Fine paintbrush

STAMENS

1 Take one white seed-head stamen and fold it in half. Cut the tips off both ends. Fold it in half and cut at the bend using fine scissors. Glue them back together with a tiny amount of non-toxic craft glue. Flatten them and leave to set. Apply a tiny amount of extra glue and then attach to the end of a half-length 26-gauge white wire. Squeeze the two together firmly, holding to about the count of ten. Repeat to make as many sets of stamen required. Allow to dry. Trim the stamens a little and then curl their tips using the sides of a small pair of scissors to run against them.

FLOWER

2 Form a ball of well-kneaded pale pink flowerpaste into a long cone shape. Pinch the broad end of the cone into a 'wizard's hat' shape. Place the brim of the hat against the non-stick board and roll out the base using the celstick to thin it out and create a tight waistline around the thicker area of the shape.

3 Place the dianthus cutter over the thick area of the shape and cut out the flower, scrubbing the cutter against the board to create a good cut edge. Remove the shape from the cutter and place back against the board.

4 Use the celstick to broaden and thin each petal, leaving the central part of each petal slightly thicker. Next, use the broad end of the Dresden tool to thin the top edge of each petal, pulling the paste against the board, which will both thin and give a slightly frilled edge.

5 Pick up the flower and open up the centre using the pointed end of the celstick. Next, use fine scissors to snip into the edges of the petals to create the fringed edge.

6 Moisten the base of the stamens with fresh egg white and thread through the centre of the flower, leaving the tips of the curled stamens slightly proud of the top of the flower. Work the back of the flower between your finger and thumb to thin it down into a slender neck. Trim off any excess. Pinch the base of each petal from behind to create a little movement in the petals. Flick the edges to create more movement in the fringed edges. Go back and add extra snips if needed.

CALYX

7 This can be cut out using a fine calyx cutter or, for a quick finish, the paste behind the flower can be snipped with fine scissors to create the five sepals. Add two snips at the very base of the calyx to create the characteristic scale shape.

BUD

8 Insert a half-length of 28-gauge white wire into the base of a cone-shaped piece of pale pink flowerpaste. Thin down the shape to create a slender bud shape. Pinch three flanges from the tip of the bud to represent the outer three petals. Keep pinching to thin out each petal and then twist the petals back onto themselves to create a spiralled petal formation. Snip the calyx as described for the flower.

LEAVES

9 Cut short lengths of 33-gauge white wire. Attach a small ball of pale holly/ivy flowerpaste onto the end of the wire and blend it onto the wire to create a fine, slender leaf shape. Place the shape against the non-stick board and flatten it using the flat/plain side of any of your leaf/petal veiners. Trim the leaf if needed using scissors or the plain-edge cutting wheel. Soften the edges and then pinch a central vein from the base to the tip. Curve slightly. Repeat to make numerous leaves, bearing in mind that the leaves always occur in pairs.

COLOURING AND ASSEMBLY

10 Dust the flower petals and buds with plum petal dust. Add a touch of white to calm down the pink if required. The backs of the petals and the buds are a much paler pink than the upper surface of the petals.

11 Use a fine paintbrush and cyclamen liquid food colour to add detailed markings at the base of each petal to create a decorative eye. Use a touch of white petal dust diluted with clear alcohol at the very centre of the flower.

12 Dust the leaves and the calyces with a light mixture of foliage and white petal dusts mixed together. Add tinges of aubergine at the tips of the leaves and base of the calyx if desired.

13 Tape the leaves in pairs onto each flower and bud stem using quarter-width nile green floristry tape. Dust the stems to match the calyx and leaves.

Rose

Roses (*Rosa*) are the most requested flower for bridal work and for cake decorators too!
There are several methods for creating roses – the method described here
is the style that I prefer and use most often.

EQUIPMENT

Fine-nose pliers
Non-stick rolling pin
Rose petal cutter set (TT549, 550, 551)
Foam pad
Metal ball tool (CC)
Very large rose petal veiner (SKGI)
Cornflour bag (p 11)
Plastic food bag
Smooth ceramic tool or cocktail stick
Kitchen paper ring former (p 11)
Dusting brushes
Non-stick board
Curved scissors
Grooved board
Rose leaf cutter (Jem)
Large briar rose leaf veiner (SKGI)
Set of three black rose leaf cutters (Jem)

MATERIALS

30-, 28-, 26-, and 18-gauge white wires
Nile green floristry tape
White and holly/ivy flowerpaste
Fresh egg white
Vine, edelweiss, daffodil, sunflower, moss, foliage,
forest, aubergine, plum and ruby petal dusts
Edible spray varnish or half glaze (p 12)

ROSE CONE CENTRE

1 Tape over a half to three-quarter length of 18-gauge white wire with half-width nile green floristry tape. Bend a large open hook in the end using fine-nose pliers. Form a ball of well-kneaded white flowerpaste into a cone shape to measure about two-thirds the length of the smallest rose petal cutter you are planning to use. Moisten the hook with fresh egg white and insert into the rounded base of the cone. Push the hook into most of the length of the cone. Pinch the base of the flowerpaste onto the wire to secure the two together. Reshape the point of the cone if required – I tend to form a sharp point with a more rounded base. Allow to dry for as long as possible.

2 Colour a large amount of white flowerpaste to the required colour; here I have used vine green petal dust to give a soft off-white base colour. I usually colour the paste paler than I want the finished rose to be.

FIRST AND SECOND LAYERS

3 Roll out some of the coloured flowerpaste fairly thinly using a non-stick rolling pin. Cut out four petals using the smaller of the two rose petal cutters you are planning to use. Place the petals on the foam pad and soften the edges using the metal ball tool – work half on the edge of the petal and half on the pad using a rolling action with the tool. Try not to frill the edges; at this stage you are only taking away the raw cut edge of the petal. Vein each of the petals in turn using the double-sided very large rose petal veiner – dust with a little cornflour if needed to prevent sticking, especially if your veiner is being used for the first time. For smaller roses it is not always essential to vein the petals but the larger flowers benefit from it greatly.

4 Place the first petal against the dried cone using a little fresh egg white to help stick it in place. It needs to be positioned quite high against the cone so that you have enough of the petal to curl tightly to form a spiral effect around the cone. It is important that this cone is not visible from the overview of the finished rose. Do not worry about covering the cone near the base – there are plenty more petals to follow that will do that job. I tend to curl the petal in from the left-hand side. Leave the right-hand edge of the petal slightly open so that the next petal can be tucked underneath it.

5 Moisten the remaining three petals with fresh egg white and start the second layer by tucking a petal underneath the first petal on the cone. Stick down the edge of the first petal over the new petal. Place the next petal over the join created and then turn the rose to add the third petal. I tend to keep these petals open to start with so that I can get the positioning correct before tightening them around the cone to form a spiral shape. Leave one of the petals open slightly to take the first petal of the next layer. Some roses have slightly pinched petals – this can be done as you add each layer by pinching the top edge to create a slight point. This number of petals can be used to make small rosebuds but the cone base should be made slightly smaller so that the petals cover the whole of it.

THIRD, FOURTH AND FIFTH LAYERS

6 Roll out some more coloured flowerpaste and cut out nine petals using the same size cutter as before. Soften the edges and vein the petals as before. Cover the petals with a plastic food bag to stop them drying out – otherwise it is a case of cutting out and working on only three petals at a time.

Tuck the first petal underneath the open petal from the previous layer of the rosebud and continue to add the other petals as described above, attaching them in layers of three petals at a time. It is important to keep positioning petals over joins in the previous layer and not to line up petals directly behind each other. Gradually start to loosen the petals slightly as you work on the fourth and fifth layers. Pinch and curl the edges slightly more as you attach the fifth layer.

SIXTH LAYER

7 Roll out some more coloured flowerpaste and cut out three petals using the slightly larger rose petal cutter. Soften and vein as before. This time, start to hollow out the centre of each petal using a large ball tool or by simply rubbing the petal with your thumb.

8 Moisten the base of each petal with fresh egg white, creating a 'V' shape. Attach to the rose as before, trying to place each petal over a join in the previous layer. Pinch either side of the petal at the base as you attach them so that it retains the cupped shape and allows the rose to breathe. Curl back the edges using the smooth ceramic tool, a cocktail stick or just your fingers to create more movement in the petal edges. I tend to curl either edge of the petal to create a more pointed petal shape. At this stage you have made what is termed a 'half rose'.

FINAL LAYER

9 I prefer to wire the petals individually for the final layer of the rose; this gives more movement and also a much stronger finished flower. Roll out some coloured flowerpaste, leaving a subtle ridge down the centre. Cut out the petal using the same size cutter as for the previous layer. Hook and moisten the end of a 26-gauge white wire. Insert it into the very base of the ridge. Soften the edges and vein as described previously. You will need cornflour dusting onto either the petal or the veiner

at this stage to prevent the flowerpaste sticking to the veiner. Press the veiner firmly to create stronger veins. Remove from the veiner and hollow out the centre using your thumb and also start to curl back the edges. Allow the petal to dry slightly in a kitchen paper ring former. Repeat to make about eight to ten petals; the number varies with each rose that I make. As the petals are beginning to firm up, you can keep going back to add extra curls to the edges if required.

ASSEMBLY AND COLOURING

10 I prefer to tape the individually wired petals around the half rose and then dust the rose as a whole – I balance the colour better this way. You might prefer to dust and then tape. It is best if the petals are not quite dry at this stage so that you can reshape and manipulate them. Tape the first wired petal over a join in the petals of the half rose using half-width nile green floristry tape. The next petal is placed onto the opposite side of the rose and then I continue adding the petals to cover gaps and joins in the previous layer. As before, try not to place petals in line with petals of the layer underneath.

11 Mix together edelweiss, vine, daffodil and sunflower petal dusts. Probe the flower with a brush loaded with this mix to add a 'glow' at the base of each petal on the back and front. I tend to be heavier with this colour on the back of the petals. The rose pictured has been dusted lightly with a very light mixture of vine, moss and edelweiss petal dusts.

CALYX

12 As the outer petals of the rose have been individually wired I find it is best to wire each sepal of the calyx too. This gives a stronger finish but also allows the flower-maker to represent a calyx with very long, slender sepals. A quicker calyx may be added using a rose calyx cutter if time or patience won't allow a wired calyx. Cut five lengths of 28-gauge white wire. Work a ball of holly/ivy flowerpaste onto the wire creating a long, tapered carrot shape. Place the shape against the non-stick board and flatten using the flat side of one of the double-sided veiners. If the shape looks distorted, simply trim into shape with a pair of scissors.

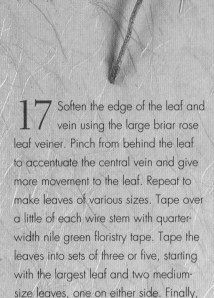

13 Place the flattened shape onto the foam pad or the palm of your hand, and soften and hollow out the length using the metal ball tool. Pinch the sepal from the base to the tip. Cut fine 'hairs' into the edge of the sepal using curved scissors. Repeat to make five sepals. I tend to leave one sepal without hairs – although remember there are some varieties of rose that have no hairs to their calyces at all.

14 Dust each sepal on the outer surface with a mixture of foliage and forest green. Add tinges of aubergine mixed with plum or ruby petal dust. Use the same brush used for the green mixture and dust lightly on the inner surface of each sepal with edelweiss petal dust. Lightly glaze the back of each sepal with edible spray varnish or half glaze.

15 Tape the five sepals to the base of the rose, positioning a sepal over a join. Add a ball of flowerpaste for the ovary and pinch and squeeze it into a neat shape. Some florists' roses have almost no ovary – they have been bred out to prolong the life of the cut flower. Dust and glaze to match the sepals.

LEAVES

16 I don't often use rose leaves as foliage in bridal bouquets, however, they are essential for arrangements. Rose leaves on commercial florists' roses tend to grow in sets of three or five. I generally make one large, two medium and two small for each set. Roll out some holly/ivy flowerpaste, leaving a thick ridge for the wire (a grooved board can speed up this process greatly). Cut out the leaves using the rose leaf cutters. I like the shape of the black rose leaf set of cutters, however, these do not allow you to roll the paste too thickly as they are shallow and the paste often sticks to them. You just need to ignore this and carry on working. Insert a 30-, 28- or 26-gauge white wire moistened with fresh egg white into the leaf, depending on its size. I usually insert the wire about half way into the ridge.

17 Soften the edge of the leaf and vein using the large briar rose leaf veiner. Pinch from behind the leaf to accentuate the central vein and give more movement to the leaf. Repeat to make leaves of various sizes. Tape over a little of each wire stem with quarter-width nile green floristry tape. Tape the leaves into sets of three or five, starting with the largest leaf and two medium-size leaves, one on either side. Finally, add the two smaller leaves at the base.

18 Dust the edges with aubergine and plum or ruby petal dusts mixed together. Use this colour on the upper stems too. Dust the upper surface of the leaf in layers lightly with forest green and more heavily with foliage and vine green. Dust the backs with edelweiss using the brush used for the greens. Spray with edible spray varnish.

Rose hips

Rose hips, with their wonderful shape, size and colour variations, make them a very welcome decorative fruit addition to floral displays and cake designs.

STAMENS AND CALYX

1 Part two fingers and then wrap 120-gauge lace maker's thread around them several times – the number will depend on the size/type of hip you are making. Remove the loop from your fingers and twist into a figure of eight shape and then fold in half to produce a smaller loop. Bend a length of 24-gauge white wire through the centre of the loop and tape over tightly with half-width nile green floristry tape. Repeat this process at the opposite side of the loop to create two sets of stamens. Cut through the centre using scissors. Trim shorter as required.

2 Fluff up the tips of the stamens by rubbing the thread against an emery board. Dust with nutkin and a touch of black petal dusts. To create a more decayed finish, simply hold the stamens over a naked flame to singe the tips very slightly.

3 To make the calyx, follow the steps for the rose calyx (see steps 12 to 15, pages 34–5) to make five sepals. Tape the sepals around the thread using half-width nile green floristry tape. Dust each sepal with a light mixture of foliage and vine green petal dusts. Catch the tips and edges with a mixture of ruby and aubergine. The inside of each sepal benefits from a light dusting of white petal dust.

HIP

4 Roll a ball of pale green flowerpaste to the desired size and shape. Pull the wired calyx/stamens through the ball using a very small amount of fresh egg white to secure them together.

5 Dust the hip before the paste starts to dry. Here I have used tangerine, ruby, vine green and tinges of foliage green petal dusts. Allow to dry and then spray in layers with edible spray varnish until you achieve the desired glossy finish. Follow steps 16 to 18 on page 35 to make the rose leaves.

MATERIALS
120-gauge lace maker's thread (APOC)
24-gauge white wire
Nile green floristry tape
Nutkin, black, foliage, vine, ruby, aubergine white and tangerine petal dusts
Pale green flowerpaste
Fresh egg white
Edible spray varnish

EQUIPMENT
Scissors
Emery board
Dusting brushes
Rose leaf cutters (Jem)
Large briar rose leaf veiner (SKGI)

Asparagus

The asparagus family contains around 130 species and also includes the asparagus fern and smilax, prized by florists and flower arrangers for their decorative foliage. However, it is the shoots of *Asparagus officinalis* that have been cultivated and eaten since ancient Egyptian times.

MATERIALS

22- or 20-gauge white wires
Pale green flowerpaste
Fresh egg white
Vine, foliage, aubergine, African violet and plum petal dusts
Edible spray varnish

EQUIPMENT

Wire cutters
Small fine scissors
Dresden tool
Plain-edge cutting wheel
Dusting brushes

SHOOT

1 Cut a length of 22- or 20-gauge white wire, depending on the size and thickness of asparagus you are planning to make. Here, I have used the finer wire to make slender and small asparagus shoots. Roll a ball of well-kneaded pale green flowerpaste and then apply pressure to one side of the ball to turn it into a cone shape.

2 Insert a wire moistened with fresh egg white, and quickly and firmly work the paste down the wire between your finger and thumb to create the required thickness and length. Keep a smaller cone shape present at the tip of the wire. Smooth the length of the paste between your palms.

3 Next, use small fine scissors to snip tiny scales into the tip of the shoot. Gradually increase the size of the scales as you work towards the base of the small cone shape.

4 Form several teardrops of pale green flowerpaste and flatten them. Thin out slightly if needed and then mark a central vein using the fine end of the Dresden tool. Repeat to make scales varying in size a little as you work. Attach these scales to the asparagus stem, gradually increasing the size and also the spacing as you work down the stem.

5 Add some fine veins to the length of the shoot using the plain-edge cutting wheel. Curve the shoot slightly.

6 Dust with a mix of vine and foliage green petal dusts. Fade the colour towards the base of the shoot. Add tinges of aubergine and African violet to each of the scales. Use a light dusting of plum at the base of the shoot. Spray lightly with edible spray varnish or steam to remove the dry-dusted appearance left by the colour.

Radish

I adore radishes and have been wanting to make them in sugar or cold porcelain for several years now, so here at last, is my version of this beautiful vegetable. There are about three species of radish (*Raphanus*) originating in Europe and western Asia. The cultivated varieties provide a wonderful range of colours, shapes and sizes.

MATERIALS

26- and 28-gauge white wires
Pale green and white flowerpaste
Fresh egg white
Foliage, vine, kiko, racy red, plum, ruby and aubergine petal dusts
Nile green floristry tape
Fine fibre from a sweetcorn, fine lace maker's thread, or sisal (optional)
Hi-tack non-toxic craft glue (optional)
Edible spray varnish

EQUIPMENT

Fresh radish leaves
Silicone plastique
Scissors or wire cutters
Rose petal cutters (TT)
Non-stick board
Dresden tool
Radish leaf veiner set (homemade or Aldaval)
Dusting brushes

LEAVES

I made my own veiners using fresh radish leaves and food-grade silicone plastique as at the time of writing this book there are no commercial radish leaf veiners available. It is very satisfying being able to take a direct copy of the real thing and it also means that your own set of veiners is fairly unique too! (See p 10 for more details about making your own petal and leaf veiners.)

1 To make the fleshy stems of the leaves it is best to make them in advance so that they can dry a little before inserting into the leaf shape.

Cut a half-length of 26-gauge white wire and blend a small ball of pale green flowerpaste onto the dry wire, trying to leave the stem broader at the base and finer at the tip of the wire. The length of this fleshy stem varies, as does the size of the leaves. Work the paste quickly and firmly between your finger and thumb to coat the wire and then place in the fleshy part of your palms to roll and smooth the stem. Repeat to make the required number of stems. I usually use between three and five leaves per radish.

2 Next, roll out some pale green flowerpaste, leaving a thick ridge at the centre to hold the wire. Cut out the leaf shape using one of the rose petal cutters. Insert the tip of the fleshy-coated wire into the pointed end of the rose petal shape. Pinch the paste down onto the stem to secure a good, strong join. Some radish leaves have side sections too – these can sometimes be simply pinched from the base of the leaf between your finger and thumb. For larger side sections simply add extra pinched pieces of flowerpaste at the base of the upper leaf. A touch of fresh egg white might be needed to secure the two together.

3 Place the leaf down against the non-stick board and work the edge of the leaf with the broad end of the Dresden tool to create more of the untidy edge character that the leaves have. Pull the edges of the leaf at intervals down against the board. Don't forget the side sections too.

4 Place the leaf into an appropriate sized double-sided radish leaf veiner and press firmly to texture the surface. Remove from the veiner and pinch from the base of the leaf to the tip to accentuate the central veiner. Allow to firm up over a gentle curve. Repeat to make the required number of leaves.

5 Dust each leaf in layers with foliage and vine petal dusts. Keep the back of the leaves and the base of the stalk slightly paler.

6 Tape a group of leaves together using half-width nile green floristry tape. Trim the wires slightly before inserting into the main body of the radish.

RADISH

7 Roll a ball of well-kneaded white flowerpaste. Work the ball into a rounded teardrop shape. Insert the taped group of leaves into the rounded end of the teardrop and carefully squeeze and blend the main body of the radish against the foliage. Next, insert a short length of 28-gauge white wire into the fine end of the radish. Carefully and firmly work the paste onto the finer wire to create a fine strand at the tip of the radish. Trim off the excess wire and flowerpaste to the required length.

ROOTS

8 The next stage is optional – use fine fibre from the inside of a sweetcorn husk or fine lace maker's thread or even a little sisal to represent the roots. Cut a few short lengths of whichever medium you decide to use and carefully glue onto the fine end of the radish. Trim away any excess threads as you work.

COLOURING

9 The colouring of a radish can vary quite a bit. Use bright pinks and reds to create the vibrant colouring. I have used kiko and racy red on the radishes illustrated – these colours are from America. You could also use plum and ruby to create an intense colour. Tinges of aubergine help to give a little depth too. Add a tinge of foliage green too, if desired, to the radish and its roots. Allow to dry before lightly spraying with edible spray varnish.

Potato vine

Potato vine (*Solanum*) produces pretty flowers in white, pink and pale lilac through to dark blue, and a few mix-and-matches in between too. The plant also produces attractive berries that ripen from green through to yellow and red, and in some cases through to black. The trailing nature of the plant makes it an ideal addition to floral displays.

MATERIALS

Melon, white and pale green flowerpaste
33-, 30-, 28-, 26- and 22-gauge white wires
Small seed-head stamens
Daffodil, sunflower, foliage, African violet, white, plum, vine, aubergine and black petal dusts
Fresh egg white
Nile green floristry tape
Edible spray varnish

EQUIPMENT

Scissors
Plain-edge cutting wheel or scalpel
Dusting brushes
Celstick or smooth ceramic tool (HP)
Small calyx cutter (TT)
Ball tool
Tiny blossom cutter (Kemper)
Non-stick rolling pin
Simple leaf cutters (TT)
Bittersweet leaf veiner (SKGI)
Fine scissors

STAMENS

1 Attach a small cigar-shaped piece of melon-coloured flowerpaste onto the end of a 28-gauge white wire. Insert a short cut piece of a small seed-head stamen into the end to represent the pistil. Divide the flowerpaste into five sections using the plain-edge cutting wheel or a scalpel to represent the stamens. Dust with a mixture of daffodil and sunflower petal dusts.

PETALS

2 Pinch a ball of well-kneaded white flowerpaste to leave a raised 'pimple' at the centre. Thin out around the 'pimple' using a rolling action with a celstick or smooth ceramic tool. Cut out the flower shape using the small calyx cutter.

3 Elongate each petal very slightly and then roll each edge of the petals to broaden them with the smooth ceramic tool. Hollow out the back of each petal a little using the small end of the ball tool.

4 Pinch a central vein down each petal to accentuate a central vein. Moisten the base of the stamens with fresh egg white and thread through the centre of the flower. Pinch the pimple behind the flower to secure it in place.

5 Add a small calyx if time allows using the tiny blossom cutter and pale green flowerpaste. Thread and attach behind the petals. Otherwise, simply dust behind the flower with some foliage petal dust (not if entering competitions though!).

6 Leave to dry and then apply the petal dust as desired. Here I have used a very light mixture of African violet, white and plum petal dusts. Tape over each flower stem and then tape them into clusters using quarter-width nile green floristry tape.

LEAVES

7 Roll out some pale green flowerpaste, leaving a thick ridge for the wire. Cut out the leaf using one of the sizes of simple leaf cutters. Moisten a 30-, 28- or 26-gauge white wire with fresh egg white and insert it into the length (the gauge will depend on the size of leaf you are making). Soften the edge of the leaf with the ball tool and then texture using the bittersweet leaf veiner.

8 Pinch the leaf from the base to the tip to accentuate the central vein. Repeat to make numerous leaves in graduating sizes. Dust the leaves with foliage and vine petal dusts. Add a tinge of African violet mixed with aubergine on the edge. Spray lightly with edible spray varnish. Tape over each leaf stem with quarter-width nile green floristry tape.

BERRIES

9 Roll several balls of pale green flowerpaste and then form each into an egg shape. Insert a 33- or 30-gauge white wire into each fruit so that the wire almost pierces through the pointed end. Add a calyx as for the flower or add a quick-snipped five sepal calyx using fine scissors. Repeat to maker numerous berries in varying sizes.

10 Tape over each stem with quarter-width nile green floristry tape and then form small clusters of berries. Dust the berries in varying degrees of vine, aubergine and finally black petal dusts. Allow to dry and then spray with edible spray varnish.

11 Tape a few smaller leaves onto a 22-gauge white wire using half-width nile green floristry tape, alternating and graduating them down the stem. Introduce clusters of flowers or berries at a leaf axle. Dust the stems with aubergine and foliage petal dusts. Curve and bend the stems into shape.

Pink brunia

There are about seven species of Brunia from South Africa. At first glance, the flowers look rather like seed-heads. This variety is bright pink, making it an ideal subject for floral sugarcrafters to make. There are also grey, green and purple forms.

MATERIALS
28- and 24-gauge white wires
Pale green flowerpaste
Fresh egg white
Plum, coral, foliage, white and myrtle bridal satin petal dusts
Edible spray varnish
Nile green floristry tape

EQUIPMENT
Fine-nose pliers
Fine curved scissors
Dusting brushes

FLOWER HEAD

1 Bend a hook in the end of a 24-gauge white wire using fine-nose pliers. Roll a ball of well-kneaded pale green flowerpaste. Moisten the hooked wire with fresh egg white and insert into the ball. Pinch the base of the ball onto the wire to secure it in place.

2 Use fine curved scissors to snip into the entire surface of the ball to create a rough texture.

3 When the surface is completely textured, go back and soften the cuts slightly by pressing gently into place. Repeat to make numerous flower heads in varying sizes.

4 Dust with a mixture of plum and coral petal dusts. Use foliage green at the base and over-dust with white or myrtle bridal satin dust. Spray very lightly with edible spray varnish.

5 Tape the flower heads into groups of three and five using nile green floristry tape.

LEAVES

6 Cut short lengths of 28-gauge white wire. Roll a small ball of pale green flowerpaste and work it onto the wire to create a thickened leaf stem. Smooth it between your palms.

7 Snip over the surface of the leaf to make a 'hairy' leaf. Curve into shape. Repeat to make lots of leaves and group into sets of three and five. Dust as for the flower heads.

8 Tape the leaves in groups of three to five at the base of the flowers using half-width nile green floristry tape. Dust over the stems with foliage and myrtle bridal satin dust and tinges of the plum/coral mixture used on the flowerheads.

Peony

Peonies have been used as medicinal plants for at least two thousand years. It is thought that the plant is named after Paeon, the Greek mythological figure who was a pupil of Asclepius, the Greek god of medicine and healing. The god was jealous that Paeon had used the plant to cure a wound that Pluto had received during a fight with Hercules so he had him killed. However, Pluto was so grateful that he changed him into a Paeonia plant!

INNER PETALS

1 Roll out some pink flowerpaste, leaving a thick ridge for the wire. Cut out the petal shape using the smallest rose petal cutter.

2 Insert a 26-gauge white wire moistened with fresh egg white into the thick ridge so that it supports about half the length of the petal. Cut into the petal using fine scissors to create long, slender 'V'-shaped cuts. The number of cuts will vary as this style of peony is quite random.

3 Use the broad end of the Dresden tool to work the very edges of the petal a little and then use the ceramic silk veining tool to texture and thin out each section of the shape. Repeat to make several wired petals.

4 It is best to make a few petals at a time and dust them while the paste is still pliable so that a strong colour can be achieved easily. Here I have used plum, aubergine and kiko petal dusts.

MATERIALS

Pink and holly/ivy flowerpaste
28-, 26- and 22-gauge white wire
Fresh egg white
Plum, aubergine, kiko, foliage, vine and forest petal dusts
Nile green floristry tape
Edible spray varnish

EQUIPMENT

Non-stick rolling pin
Large rose petal cutters (set of three) (TT549-551)
Fine scissors
Dresden tool
Ceramic silk veining tool (HP)
Dusting brushes
Peony petal veiner (SKGI) (optional)
Kitchen paper ring former (p 11)
Standard rose petal cutters (TT278-280)
Ball tool
Non-stick board
Single peony leaf veiner (SKGI)
Peony leaf cutters (optional)
Scalpel

5 Again, while the petals are still pliable, start to tape them together using half-width nile green floristry tape. Pinch and fold each petal as you tape them together to create the start of the almost fluffy centre of the flower. Continue to make the petals, gradually increasing the petals in size a little as you go. The number can vary – I generally work between 20 and 50 petals for this part of the flower.

OUTER PETALS

6 Roll out some pink flowerpaste, leaving a thick ridge. Cut out a petal shape using the largest rose petal cutter. Insert a 26-gauge white wire into the ridge to support about half the length of the petal.

7 Place the petal into a double-sided peony petal veiner or texture the surface by rolling over it with the ceramic silk veining tool, turning the petal over to vein the back too. Frills are optional – some varieties have very frilly outer petals while others are quite flat. Use the ceramic silk veining tool to apply short burst of pressure at the edges of the petal, rolling to create the desired frills.

8 Cup the centre of the petal and then dry in a kitchen paper ring former. Repeat to make between six and 10 outer petals – again the number varies between varieties. Dust as for the inner petals, adding more aubergine at the base to add depth to the flower.

9 Tape these outer petals around the inner fluffy petals using half-width nile green floristry tape. It is best if these petals are still slightly pliable which will allow you to cup and shape them a little more to create a relaxed finish.

CALYX

10 There are three rounded sepal shapes to the calyx that are made using pale holy/ivy flowerpaste (add a little white flowerpaste to lighten the colour) rolled out to leave a thick ridge. Cut out the shape using one of the standard rose petal cutters – there are three sizes used here and you will need to make one sepal of each size. Insert a 28-gauge wire moistened with fresh egg white into the thick ridge at the pointed end of the shape to support about half the length. Soften the edge of the sepal and then hollow out the centre using the ball tool. Pinch a slight point at the top curved edge. Repeat to make the other two sizes.

11 As well as the rounder inner sepals, there are two or three larger leaf-like sepals too. Roll a ball of holy/ivy flowerpaste onto a 28-gauge white wire, working it into a long leaf-like shape that is pointed at both ends. Place the shape against the non-stick board and flatten it using the flat side of the peony leaf veiner. Pick up the leaf and pinch from the base to the tip to create a central vein and curve into shape. Repeat to make the second sepal so that there is a variation in length.

12 Dust the sepals with foliage and vine petal dusts mixed together. Catch the edges with a mixture of plum and aubergine.

13 Tape the three sizes of rounded sepals onto the back of the flower so that they are evenly spaced. Add the two leaf-like sepals opposite each other using half-width nile green floristry tape.

LEAVES

14 There are several sets of peony leaf cutters. I generally make one large shape with two smaller shapes to sit on either side. The leaves can be made with cutters or using a scalpel and the leaf templates on p 139. Roll out the holly/ivy flowerpaste not too thinly, leaving a thicker tapered ridge for the wire. Cut out the leaf shape and insert a wire moistened with fresh egg white – a 22-gauge for the largest leaves through to a 28-gauge for the very smallest. The wire needs to support the leaf shape as it tends to be quite fragile.

15 Soften the edge of the leaf using a large ball tool. Vein each section of the leaf with the single double-sided peony leaf veiner.

16 Pinch the leaf from the base to the tip on each section to accentuate the central veins and also to give movement to the shape. Leave to dry fairly flat with a bit of curving at the tips. Repeat to make the required number of leaves.

COLOURING

17 Dust the edges of the leaves with a mixture of aubergine and plum petal dusts. Add a tinge at the base too. Use layers of forest, foliage and vine to colour the upper surface of each leaf. Use a lighter dusting on the back of the leaves.

18 Tape into sets of three using half-width nile green floristry tape. Spray lightly with edible spray varnish.

Ornamental cabbage

These decorative cabbages are actually edible but are not as tasty as other members of the brassica family and are grown for their highly decorative quality in landscape gardening and for flower arranging.

MATERIALS
28-, 26-, 20-gauge white wire
Pale green flowerpaste
Fresh egg white
Plum, African violet, moss, forest, foliage, vine and aubergine petal dusts
Isopropyl alcohol
White floristry tape
Edible spray varnish

EQUIPMENT
Fine-nose pliers
Non-stick rolling pin
Ornamental cabbage leaf veiner set (Aldaval)
Scissors, plain-edge cutting wheel or scalpel
Dresden tool
Large ball tool
Dusting brushes
Fine paintbrush

CENTRE

1 Bend a hook in the end of a 20-gauge white wire using fine-nose pliers. Attach a ball of pale green flowerpaste onto it and leave to dry.

2 Roll out some pale green flowerpaste not too thinly and place into one of the smaller ornamental cabbage leaf veiners. Press firmly and then release it from the veiner and cut around the outline using scissors, the plain-edge cutting wheel or a scalpel. Work the edges with the Dresden tool to create a slightly untidy finish. Repeat to make several of these smaller leaves and attach around the dried wired ball using fresh egg white.

OUTER LEAVES

3 Continue making outer leaves in various sizes, leaving a thick ridge for a wire strong enough to support the size of the leaf you are working on – 28-gauge for the small leaves and 26-gauge for the larger ones. Vein as before and trim around the shape. Work the edges with the Dresden tool and soften the edges with a large ball tool. Pinch the leaf to accentuate the central vein.

COLOURING AND ASSEMBLY

4 Dust the central area of each leaf on the back and front with a mixture of plum and African violet petal dusts. Use moss, forest and foliage on the edges of the leaves with tinges of vine green here and there too. Add a little depth in places with aubergine petal dust.

5 Mix some isopropyl alcohol with plum, African violet and aubergine petal dusts and then paint a strong central vein on each leaf along with finer side veins.

6 Tape the leaves around the tight centre using half-width white floristry tape. Gradually increase the size of the leaves as you work. Dust the stem with the plum/African violet mix and also a tinge of the greens used on the foliage too.

7 Spray lightly with edible spray varnish or steam gently to set the colour.

Variegated hosta leaf

Hosta leaves are very useful leaves for the sugarcrafter to master as they are both large and decorative, filling plenty of space in a bouquet or an arrangement. There are many varieties of hosta – here a variegated form with a pink tinge is described.

LEAVES

1 Roll out the flowerpaste so that it is quite fleshy, leaving a thicker ridge for the wire. Cut out the leaf shape using the hosta leaf template on p 139 and a scalpel or plain-edge cutting wheel.

2 Insert a moistened 22- or 20-gauge white wire into the thick ridge of the leaf so that it supports at least half the length of the wire. Place the leaf onto a foam pad or in the palm of your hand if it is big enough and soften the edge using the large metal ball tool.

3 Place the leaf into a double-sided hosta leaf veiner and press firmly to texture the surface of the leaf. Remove the leaf from the veiner and then pinch the leaf from the base to the tip to accentuate the central vein. Dry curved or flatter, depending how you intend to use it in the spray or arrangement.

4 Mix together vine green, a touch of foliage and white petal dusts to colour the centre of the leaf on the back and front. Fade the colour towards the edges, leaving quite a large border of the base colour showing through. Add more depth with a mixture of foliage, white and forest petal dusts diluted with a little isopropyl alcohol. Create veins and streaks using a not too fine paintbrush. Add a tinge of plum and aubergine petal dusts to the edges if desired. Spray lightly with edible spray varnish to set the colour.

MATERIALS

Pale melon-coloured flowerpaste
22- or 20-gauge white wire
Vine, foliage, white, forest, plum and aubergine petal dusts
Isopropyl alcohol
Edible spray varnish

EQUIPMENT

Non-stick rolling pin
Scalpel or plain-edge cutting wheel
Foam pad
Large metal ball tool
Hosta leaf veiners (SKGI or Aldaval)
Dusting brushes
Paintbrush

Brassolaeliacattleya orchid

A few years ago I was invited to demonstrate at a sugarcraft exhibition in São Paulo along with my friends from the UK: Tombi Peck, Margaret Ford and David Ford. It was an intensive exhibition and one morning I was offered a quick trip to the flower market – this was just the diversion from cakes that I needed! There were hundreds of orchids as well as other flowers and plants on offer, and I was like a kid in a sweet shop! I managed to fill my hotel room with orchids and other plant material – even the mini-bar was used for storing some of the more tender flowers I had collected over the week! I managed to keep room service out of the room until all the flowers had been photographed by David Ford and then dissected by myself, Tombi and Margaret. It was a great sharing experience and kept us all entertained for days. Sadly, the following year David died, so I am very grateful for that wonderful week we all spent together in Brazil.

MATERIALS

White and green flowerpaste
26-, 24- and 22- gauge white wires
Fresh egg white
Kitchen paper ring former (p 11) or cotton wool
Nile green floristry tape
Daffodil, sunflower, white, vine, plum, African violet, foliage, forest and aubergine petal dusts
Isopropyl alcohol
Edible spray varnish

EQUIPMENT

Ceramic silk veining tool (HP)
Scalpel
Non-stick rolling pin
Amaryllis petal veiner (SKGI)
Dresden tool
Cocktail stick
Large ball tool
Non-stick board
Stargazer B petal veiner (SKGI)
Dusting brushes
Fine paintbrush
Plain-edge cutting wheel
Foam pad
Large tulip leaf veiner (SKGI)

COLUMN

This is the part of the flower that holds the throat petal (labellum). It is best if this can be made in advance and allowed to dry.

1 Roll a ball of well-kneaded white flowerpaste. Form the ball into a teardrop shape and insert a 22-gauge white wire moistened with fresh egg white into the pointed end to support about two-thirds the length of the shape.

2 Hollow out the underside of the column using the rounded smooth end of the ceramic silk veining tool. Firmly press the shape against the tool, pinching a gentle ridge down the back with your finger and thumb as you work. Curve the length of the shape. Allow to dry.

3 Add a tiny ball of white flowerpaste to represent the anther cap at the tip of the column. Divide the cap into two sections using a scalpel.

THROAT/LIP (LABELLUM)

4 Roll out some white flowerpaste, leaving a thick ridge for added support. The flowerpaste needs to be quite fleshy for this part of the flower to help create a heavily frilled throat. Cut out the throat template on p 139 using a scalpel.

5 Place the throat petal into the double-sided amaryllis petal veiner and press firmly to create a heavily veined effect.

6 Next, use the broad end of the Dresden tool to pull out the edge of the flowerpaste at intervals to create a heavy double-frilled effect. Soften the frill using the ceramic silk veining tool, again working at intervals over the frill and this time using a rolling action. The edge may also be thinned further using a cocktail stick.

7 Moisten the base of the throat petal with fresh egg white and wrap the petal around the column, making sure the column is positioned with the hollowed side down against the petal. Overlap the petal at the base and then curl back the edges slightly. There should be some space between the underside of the column and the petal – this can be corrected by opening up the area using the broad end of the Dresden tool. Leave to dry before colouring. The throat might need supporting with a kitchen paper ring former or cotton wool to hold it in place while it dries, or alternatively dry hanging upside down – checking and re-shaping as it firms to create a more relaxed finish.

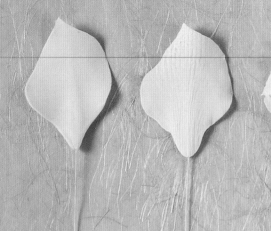

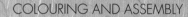

WINGS/ARMS (LATERAL PETALS)

8 Roll out some white flowerpaste, leaving a thick ridge down the centre. Cut out the petal using the wing template on p 139 and a scalpel.

9 Insert a 24-gauge white wire moistened with fresh egg white into the thick ridge so that it holds about a third to half the length of the petal. Soften the edge with the ball tool. Place into the double-sided amaryllis petal veiner and press firmly to texture it.

10 Next, place the petal against the non-stick board or rest it against your index finger to frill the edges using the ceramic silk veining tool. Pinch a subtle ridge down the centre of the petal. Repeat to make the second wing petal. Allow to dry over a gentle curve of kitchen paper.

HEAD (DORSAL SEPAL)

11 Roll out some white flowerpaste, leaving a thick ridge as before. Cut out the sepal shape using the head template on p 139 and a scalpel.

12 Insert a 26-gauge white wire moistened with fresh egg white into the thick ridge. Soften the edges using the large ball tool. Vein using the double-sided stargazer B petal veiner. Curve the sepal forwards to create a curved shape.

LEGS (LATERAL SEPALS)

13 Repeat as for the dorsal sepal to create the two lateral petals. Curve backwards to dry.

COLOURING AND ASSEMBLY

14 Tape the two wing petals onto either side of the throat petal using half-width nile green floristry tape. Next, add the dorsal sepal to curve behind the wing petals and finally the lateral sepals at the base of the flower. A concentrated mix of daffodil and sunflower petal dusts is added at the centre of the orchid throat.

15 Dust the flower as desired. Here I have used a mixture of white, daffodil and vine green petal dusts to colour the outer petals and sepals. The throat has been coloured heavily with plum, African violet and white petal dusts mixed together. A further layer of just plum has been added to intensify the petal and then a final tinge of African violet has been used on the edge. Tinge the edges of the wing petals and sepals lightly with the plum mixture. Add a light dusting of vine green and foliage to the base of the petals.

16 Dilute some plum and African violet petal dusts with isopropyl alcohol and paint a series of markings onto the throat of the orchid using a fine paintbrush. Steam the flower to set the colour and to remove the dusty finish left by using the layers of petal dust.

LEAVES

17 The leaves are fairly fleshy so try not to roll the paste too fine. Roll out some green flowerpaste, leaving a thicker ridge running down the centre for a strong gauge wire. Cut out a long leaf shape using the large end of the plain-edge cutting wheel.

18 Carefully insert a length of 22-gauge white wire into the thick ridge, supporting the paste on either side as you feed the wire into about half the length of the leaf.

19 Place the leaf onto a foam pad and then soften the edges with a large ball tool, working the tool half on the edge of the leaf and half on the pad. Do not frill the edge.

20 Next, texture the leaf using the double-sided large tulip leaf veiner. Remove from the veiner and pinch the leaf from the base to the tip to accentuate the central vein. Allow the leaf to firm up a little prior to dusting.

21 Dust the leaf in layers with forest, foliage and vine green petal dusts. Catch the edges gently with aubergine petal dust. Leave the leaf to dry before spraying with edible spray varnish.

Epigeneium orchid

There are about 35 species of epigeneium orchid that are native to India, Nepal and across Asia to the Philippines. The colour variation is vast, making it an ideal addition to the flower-maker's repertoire. The method for making them is the same as that used for a dendrobium orchid. This type of orchid, along with the dendrobium orchid, tends to be very fragile as the outer sepals are unwired so care needs to be taken when arranging them into a bouquet.

MATERIALS	EQUIPMENT
White and green flowerpaste	Ceramic silk veining tool (HP)
28-, 24- and 22-gauge white wires	Fine-nose pliers
Nile green floristry tape	Non-stick rolling pin
Fresh egg white	Curly dendrobium orchid cutter set (TT)
Small piece of sponge	Stargazer B petal veiner (SKGI)
White, African violet, plum, vine,	Non-stick board
foliage and aubergine petal dusts	Dresden tool
Edible spray varnish	Ball tool
	Fine angled tweezers
	Large scissors
	Dusting brushes
	Plain-edge cutting wheel
	Large tulip leaf veiner (SKGI)

COLUMN

1 Form a small ball of white flowerpaste into a carrot shape. This should measure about a third of the length of the dendrobium orchid lip cutter from the set. Hollow out the underside of the column by pressing it against the rounded end of the ceramic silk veining tool – pinching the back slightly as you do to create a slight ridge.

2 Tape over the length of a 24-gauge white wire with nile green floristry tape. Bend a loop in the end of the wire using fine-nose pliers. Bend the loop against the main length of wire and then hold the loop with the pliers and bend it to form a ski stick shape. Moisten the hook with fresh egg white and pull it through the centre of the column to embed it into the paste. Curve slightly and leave to dry overnight. This section must be firm enough to support and hold the rest of the flower so it is important that it is given plenty of time to dry.

LIP (LABELLUM)

3 Roll out some well-kneaded white flowerpaste quite thinly and cut out the lip shape using one of the cutters from the dendrobium orchid set.

4 Soften the edges of the petal and then vein using the stargazer B petal veiner. Next, place the petal against the non-stick board and use the broad end of the Dresden tool to double frill the edge. Soften the frill using a rolling action with the ceramic silk veining tool.

5 Hollow out the two side sections of the petal using the ball tool. Pinch two ridges at the centre of the shape using fine angled tweezers to create a raised platform.

6 Moisten the sides of the shape with fresh egg white and attach onto the dried column, hollowed-side down, against the petal. Open up the throat slightly and curl back the two side edges. Leave to set a little.

LATERAL (WING) PETALS

7 Roll out some white flowerpaste thinly, leaving a thick ridge for a fine wire. Cut out the long, narrow wing petal shape using one of the cutters from the orchid set. Carefully remove the shape from cutter. Insert a 28-gauge white wire moistened with fresh egg white into the thick ridge of the petal to support about half the length of the petal.

8 Soften the edge and then vein using the stargazer B petal veiner. Pinch the petal from the base to the tip and curve back slightly. Repeat to make a second wing petal. Tape the two wing petals onto either side of the lip and column using half-width nile green floristry tape. Place to one side.

OUTER SEPALS

9 Roll out some white flowerpaste, leaving a ridge down the centre for added support. Cut out the tri-lobed sepal shape using one of the cutters from the orchid set – line up the thick ridge so that it runs into the middle of the central petal. Remove from the cutter and then soften the edge of each section using the ball tool. Vein each sepal in turn using the stargazer B petal veiner.

10 Pinch a central vein down the centre of each sepal. Next, moisten the back and base of the wired column and lip shape with fresh egg white and then thread the wire through the centre of the shape. Ease the shape to fit onto the back of the wired sections. Position each sepal into place and firmly squeeze them onto the dried centre to keep them in place. Curl the dorsal and lateral petals forwards and then backwards towards the tips.

11 Cut a square piece of sponge and then make a slit in it using a large pair of scissors. Slide the sponge behind the flower so that it supports the outer three sepals of the orchid until they firm up enough to support their own weight. When dry remove the sponge very carefully.

COLOURING

12 Mix together white, African violet and plum petal dusts. Use this mixture to colour the inside of the lip area fading towards the edges. Dust the base of the petals and sepals using the same mixture so that the colour fades about half way down the length of each petal/sepal.

13 Use a light mixture of vine and white to colour the sepals and petals from the tip towards the centre of the orchid. Add tinges of foliage green to the tips and the very back of the orchid. Tape over the stem of each orchid with half-width nile green floristry tape to thicken each of the stems. Use fine-nose pliers to bend the stems into a graceful curve.

LEAVES

14 Roll out some green flowerpaste, leaving a thick ridge for the wire. Use the plain-edge cutting wheel to cut out a freehand not-too-slender leaf shape.

15 Insert a 24- or 22-gauge white wire moistened with fresh egg white into about half the length of the leaf. The exact gauge will depend on the size of leaf you are making.

16 Place the leaf into the double-sided large tulip leaf veiner and press the two sides together firmly to texture the surface of the leaf. Remove the leaf from the veiner and carefully pinch it from the base to the tip to accentuate the central vein. Allow to dry in a slightly curved position.

17 Dust in layers with foliage and vine green petal dusts. Catch the edges with aubergine. Allow to dry further and then lightly glaze with edible spray varnish.

Lilac

It was John Tradescant, the naturalist who became gardener to Charles I, who introduced lilac (*Syringa*) to Great Britain in 1621. Lilac is native to eastern Europe and Asia Minor. My friend, Alex Julian, kindly donated this sprig of lilac for the book – she has a lot more patience than me with tiny flowers!

BUDS

1 Cut short lengths of 33-gauge white wires. Form a ball of white flowerpaste into a cone shape. Insert a dry wire into the fine end. Thin down the neck slightly and pinch off any excess using your finger and thumb. Divide the top of the bud into four using fine scissors. Make lots of buds in varying sizes of small!

FLOWERS

2 These are made using a pulled flower method. Form a teardrop of well-kneaded white flowerpaste. Open up the broad end using the pointed end of the smooth ceramic tool.

3 Cut four sections using fine scissors. Pinch each section between your finger and thumb to form pointed petals. Next, 'pull' the petals between your finger and thumb to flatten and thin them a little.

4 Use the broad end of the Dresden tool to hollow out and mark a central vein on each petal.

5 Insert a hooked 30-gauge white wire moistened with fresh egg white through the centre of the flower. Thin the back of the flower if needed. Trim off the excess. Repeat to make numerous flowers – some should be slightly open and others fully open in shape.

COLOURING AND ASSEMBLY

6 Dust the buds and flowers as required. Here, the flowers were dusted with a mixture of empress purple, plum and African violet.

7 Tape the buds into small tight groups using quarter-width nile green floristry tape. Use these at the tip of the sprig. Continue to add other groups of flowers and buds mixed together as you work down the sprig.

MATERIALS

33- and 30-gauge white wires
White flowerpaste
Fresh egg white
Empress purple, plum and African violet petal dusts
Nile green floristry tape

EQUIPMENT

Wire cutters
Fine scissors
Smooth ceramic tool
Dresden tool
Dusting brushes

French lavender

I adore lavender. The scent is amazing and is without doubt my favourite scented plant of all time. There are many forms of lavender, with the petal-like bracts occurring in white, pink and pale blue through to strong purples and an almost black variety too. The plant is a wonderful herb that can be used to cook with and has anti-bacterial and healing qualities too.

MATERIALS

33-gauge white wire
White and pale holly/ivy flowerpaste
African violet, plum, deep purple, white,
foliage and aubergine petal dusts
Nile green floristry tape

EQUIPMENT

Wire cutters
Non-stick board
Briar rose leaf veiner (SKGI)
Dresden tool
Dusting brushes
Cocktail stick
Fine curved scissors
Fine angled tweezers

MODIFIED BRACTS

1 At first glance you could be mistaken for thinking that French lavender has large colourful petals. These are in fact modified bracts/leaves. To make the bracts, cut short lengths of 33-gauge white wire. Blend a small ball of white flowerpaste onto the wire to create a slender shape that is slightly pointed at both the base and the tip. Place the shape against the non-stick board and flatten it using the flat side of the briar rose leaf veiner. Repeat to make four bracts of varying sizes.

2 Work the edges of each bract with the broad end of the Dresden tool to create a thinned out, slightly untidy, frill effect. Next, vein each bract using the double-sided briar rose leaf veiner.

3 Pinch each bract from the base to the tip to accentuate the central vein. Curve each bract slightly.

4 Dust the bracts to the desired intensity – it is best to apply the colour before the paste dries to create a strong effect. Here I have used a mixture of African violet, plum and deep purple petal dusts. Fade the colour towards the edge a little.

5 Tape the four bracts together with quarter-width nile green floristry tape, making sure that the ridged veins of the back of each bract are facing the outer edges. If the paste is still pliable you will find that now is a good time to reshape the bracts to create a more relaxed/realistic effect.

FLOWERS AND BUDS

6 These are tiny and not always in flower, so you might prefer not to make them. I have only used buds in the lavender illustrated here and if I am making flowers, then I tend to create very simple, almost abstract, forms, as to create an accurate replica takes too much time. For the buds, form tiny sausage shapes of African violet-coloured flowerpaste. Taper both ends. Make lots and leave to set hard. For the flowers, hollow out the broad end of a tiny cone of African violet-coloured flowerpaste using a cocktail stick. Thin the edges at intervals with the Dresden tool to create a five-petal effect. Leave to dry.

GREEN BRACTS/CALYX

7 Attach a ball of pale holly/ivy flowerpaste at the base of the wired bracts. Blend the paste into a tight waistline where it meets the base of the bracts. Elongate and thin the base of the green paste too and remove any excess. The size and shape of this green section can vary quite a bit. I have kept it fairly slender in my sugar version to create a daintier effect for cake decorating purposes.

8 Use fine curved scissors to snip a scale effect into the surface of the green flowerpaste – this is to represent the numerous green bracts that occur in this section. Add a few pinched lines with fine angled tweezers onto each bract.

9 Before the flowerpaste dries, quickly insert the required amount of dried buds and flowers into the paste so that they appear out of the bract shapes. Leave to dry before colouring.

10 Dust the whole of the green bract shape with a mixture of white and foliage petal dusts. Add tinges of African violet mixed with aubergine. Dust the buds and flowers as desired – these can be a clean purple through to an almost dark purple-black colour.

LEAVES

11 Cut several short lengths of 33-gauge white wire. Attach a tiny ball of pale holly/ivy flowerpaste onto the end of a dry wire and work the paste onto the wire to create a fine strand shape. Flatten the shape against the non-stick board using the flat side of the briar rose leaf veiner. Soften the edge if needed and then pinch from the base to the tip to create a central vein. Repeat to make the leaves in pairs.

12 Tape the leaves in pairs down the stem of the lavender using quarter-width nile green floristry tape. Dust the stem to match the green bract/calyx. Steam to set the colour.

Purple chilli peppers

Most people are familiar with green, yellow and red chillies, and while these are great to use in cake designs, the decorative purple chillies provide an added unusual interest to floral displays. Chilli peppers originate from Spain, east and west Africa, Thailand and tropical India, and belong to the **Solanaceae** family, which also includes the potato, tomato and aubergine.

MATERIALS

Small white seed-head stamens
28-, 26-, 24- and 20-gauge white wires
Hi-tack non-toxic craft glue
Sunflower, African violet, plum, forest, vine, foliage and aubergine petal dusts
White and pale green flowerpaste
Fresh egg white
Edible spray varnish
Fresh chilli
Nile green floristry tape

EQUIPMENT

Dusting brushes
Non-stick board
Celstick or smooth ceramic tool (HP)
Six-petal pointed blossom cutter (OPN6)
Dresden tool
Fine scissors
Fine-nose pliers
Scalpel
Plain-edge cutting wheel
Bittersweet leaf veiner (SKGI)
Silicone plastique
Fine angled tweezers

STAMENS

1 Attach six short white seed-head stamens to the end of a 26-gauge white wire using non-toxic craft glue. Allow to dry before dusting lightly with sunflower and a tinge of African violet petal dusts. The stamens and petals of the flower of the purple chilli are also purple. If you are making green, yellow, orange or red chillies, then the stamens are yellow with pure white petals to the flower.

FLOWER

2 Form a teardrop of well-kneaded white flowerpaste and then pinch the broad end of the cone into a hat shape. Place the shape onto a non-stick board and roll out the edges with a celstick or smooth ceramic tool, forming a neat waistline as you work.

3 Use the six-petal pointed blossom cutter to cut out the flower shape. Place the flower flat onto the non-stick board and elongate and broaden each petal slightly using a rolling action. Open up the centre of the flower using the pointed end of the celstick or smooth ceramic tool. Place the flower on your index finger and create a hollowed-out vein effect using the broad end of the

Dresden tool. Next, pinch the tips of each petal into a sharp point. Moisten the base of the stamens with fresh egg white and pull through the centre of the flower. Remove any excess flowerpaste using fine scissors or your finger and thumb as you thin down the back with your fingers. Add a calyx. Dust the petal edges with a mixture of African violet and plum.

BUDS

4 Form a cone shape of white flowerpaste. Insert a hooked 28-gauge white wire into the broad end of the cone and then work the base down on to the wire to form a more slender neck shape. Divide the tip into six sections using a scalpel or fine scissors. Add a small calyx as described in step 7. Colour as for the flower.

LEAVES

5 Roll out some pale green flowerpaste, leaving a thick ridge for the wire. Cut out a basic leaf shape using the plain-edge cutting wheel. Insert a 26- or 24-gauge white wire into about half the length of the thick ridge. Soften the edge and then vein using the bittersweet leaf veiner. Pinch the leaf down the centre to accentuate the central vein. Curve slightly and allow to firm before dusting with layers of forest, vine and foliage petal dusts. Spray lightly with edible spray varnish.

CHILLIES

6 It's best to make a mould with silicone plastique from a real fresh chilli (see p 10 for more details about making your own petal and leaf veiners).

Form a ball of well-kneaded pale green flowerpaste into a long, slender chilli shape, smoothing the shape between the padded part of your palms. Insert a hooked 24-gauge white wire moistened with fresh egg white and then texture the surface by pushing the shape into the homemade chilli mould. Remove and curve slightly.

CALYX

7 Form a small cone-shaped piece of pale green flowerpaste and hollow out the broader end using the rounded end of the smooth ceramic tool or celstick. Moisten the centre and thread onto the back of the chilli, thinning down the paste onto the wire to create a fine elongated stem. Pinch six sepals using fine angled tweezers. Dust the calyx with foliage and vine green.

COLOURING AND ASSEMBLY

8 It is best to dust the chillies before they have a chance to dry. Dust the smaller green chillies with vine and foliage green. Use African violet, plum and aubergine in layers for the more mature chillies. Allow to dry before spraying with a few layers of edible spray varnish.

9 Using half-width nile green floristry tape, tape the flowers and buds into small groups, with the odd small green chilli too. Tape the more colourful matured chillies into groups. Tape the various groups of flowers and chillies onto a 20-gauge white wire using half-width nile green floristry tape and adding leaves alternating down the stem as you work.

White bombax

There are eight species of bombax tree native to India and the drier parts of Burma. The flowers are very large and the petals vary in width and length between varieties. There are also red and orange forms. Usually, the white bombax has narrower petals than its coloured counterparts but I have used a little artistic licence here, preferring the broader petals of the red and orange varieties. The tree also produces a fruit, which when ripe, splits to reveal a silky material similar to that from the kapok tree which is often used for stuffing cushions. These flowers are very useful for filling spaces in floral displays and create maximum impact too.

MATERIALS

White and green cold porcelain

26-, 24-, 22-, 20- and 18-gauge white wires

White seed-head stamens

Hi-tack non-toxic craft glue

Vine, sunflower, white, plum, foliage, aubergine, forest, nutkin, tangerine and coral petal dusts

Isopropyl alcohol

White and holly/ivy flowerpaste

Fresh egg white

Nile green and brown floristry tape

Edible spray varnish

Kitchen paper

Tangerine paste food colour

EQUIPMENT

Fine scissors

Fine angled tweezers

Dusting brushes

Fine paintbrushes

Non-stick rolling pin

Amaryllis cutter (TT748)

Large metal ball tool

Stargazer B petal veiner (SKGI)

Rose petal cutter set (TT276-280)

Fine-nose pliers

Plain-edge cutting wheel

Large gardenia leaf veiner (SKGI or Aldaval)

Large scissors

PISTIL AND STAMENS

To create a neat centre it is best to use a non-toxic craft glue to hold the stamens and pistil together – because of this I prefer to make the pistil with cold porcelain as the glue bonds far easier than it would with flowerpaste.

1 Form a ball of white cold porcelain and insert a 24-gauge white wire. Leaving a slightly rounded tip to the pistil, work the paste down onto the wire to cover about 5 cm (2 in). Smooth the length of the pistil, working it between the fleshy part of your palms. Gently curve the pistil. Next, divide the bulbous tip into five sections using fine scissors. Open up the five sections and carefully pinch each section between your finger and thumb to neaten them and then curl them back slightly. Attach a ball of green cold porcelain at the base of the pistil and work into an oval shape.

2 Next, you will need at least one to two full bunches of seed-head stamens. Divide the bunches into groups of about 15 stamens and line up their tips. Use a small amount of non-toxic craft glue to bond one end of each bunch together. Allow to dry for several minutes. Try not to use too much glue as this will take much longer to dry. Clean the excess glue from your fingers before trimming off the excess stamens from the glued end. You might need to shorten the groups, bearing in mind that the pistil should stand slightly higher than the stamens. Once the stamens are dry enough, simply apply a touch more glue to the glued ends and then attach to the green ovary at the base of the pistil. Continue to add more groups of stamen until the desired effect is achieved – some flowers have larger, bushier stamens than others. Leave to dry, then curl back the stamens slightly using fine angled tweezers.

3 Dust the stamens from the base fading towards the tips with a light dusting of vine green petal dust. Next, dilute some sunflower petal dust with isopropyl alcohol and carefully paint the tips of each of the stamens using the fine paintbrush. As the flower fades, the stamens have brown tinges to them – but with a white flower I prefer to keep the stamens a fresh yellow colour.

PETALS

4 Now back to using flowerpaste! Roll out some well-kneaded white flowerpaste, leaving a thick ridge for the wire. The petals of this flower are quite fleshy so be careful not to roll too heavily. Use the amaryllis cutter to cut out the petal shape. Insert a 26-gauge white wire moistened with fresh egg white into about half the length of the petal. Soften the edge of the petal using the large ball tool – try not to frill the petals.

5 Place the petal into the double-sided stargazer B petal veiner and squeeze firmly to create strong veining. Remove from the veiner and then pinch the petal from the base to the tip to accentuate the central vein and also to curve the shape slightly. Repeat the process to create five petals.

COLOURING AND ASSEMBLY

6 Dust the base of each petal with a mixture of vine green and white petal dusts. Tinge the back of each petal down the centre and at the tips with this light mixture too. Add delicate tinges to the side edges using a light mixture of plum and white petal dusts if desired.

7 It is best to tape the petals around the stamens with half-width nile green floristry tape while they are still slightly pliable so that you may reshape them slightly and create a more realistic balanced result. The back of the flower is quite bulbous so at this stage you will need to attach a ball of holly/ivy flowerpaste over the base of the petals to create a padded finish which will then be covered by the sepals of the calyx.

CALYX

8 Roll out some holly/ivy flowerpaste not too thinly and cut out three large rose petal shapes using the largest rose petal cutter. Soften the edges and cup the centre of each sepal using the large metal ball tool. Attach over the padded base of the flower using fresh egg white. Pinch the tip of each sepal into a sharp point. Dust with vine and foliage petal dusts.

BUDS

9 Bend an open hook in the end of a 20-gauge white wire using fine-nose pliers. Form a cone shape of well-kneaded white flowerpaste and insert the hooked wire moistened with fresh egg white into the rounded base. Pinch five petals from the sides of the cone using your finger and thumb – you might need a pair of fine angled tweezers too to get tight into the base of each petal. Keep pinching each of the petals to make them finer. Next, twist to spiral the petals around the bud. Add a calyx as described for the flower, using a slightly smaller rose petal cutter.

LEAVES

10 Roll out some holly/ivy flowerpaste, leaving a thick ridge for the wire. Cut out a long, pointed freestyle leaf shape using the plain-edge cutting wheel. Insert a moistened 26- or 24-gauge white wire into about half the length of the leaf – the gauge will depend on the size of the leaf you are making. Next, work the thick base of the leaf between your finger and thumb to elongate it and create a thickened stem. Repeat to make leaves in varying sizes.

11 Soften the edge of the leaf and then place it into the double-sided large gardenia leaf veiner and press firmly to texture the leaf. Remove from the veiner and then pinch from the base to the tip to accentuate the central vein. Repeat to make five leaves for each set of foliage.

12 Tape the five leaves together to form a hand-like formation using half-width nile green floristry tape.

COLOURING

13 Dust the edges of each leaf with aubergine petal dust. Use layers of forest, foliage and vine to colour the main body of the leaves. Dust the back of the leaves much lighter than the front. Tape the group onto an extra 22-gauge white wire to give support using half-width nile green floristry tape. Spray lightly with edible spray varnish.

ASSEMBLY

14 If you wish to create a branch of bombax, simply tape the flowers, buds and foliage onto 18-gauge white wire. Thicken the branch using strips of kitchen paper wrapped around the wire and tape over with brown floristry tape. Smooth the stem using the side of a large pair of scissors to polish it. Every time you add a flower or a bud, add a set of leaves too. To create added texture, twist some brown floristry tape back onto itself to form a long strand. Wrap this around the branch at intervals, focusing mostly at the base of the buds, flowers and leaves.

15 Dust the branch with nutkin petal dust and spray lightly with edible spray varnish.

ORANGE FLOWERS

16 If you decide to make the orange form featured here, then you will need to colour the paste with some tangerine paste food colour to form the base colouring and then over-dust with tangerine and coral petal dusts. The stamens' tips are coloured with nutkin rather than sunflower yellow petal dust and the calyx is often a stronger brown/aubergine colour. There are also red forms of bombax; for these, use red-coloured flowerpaste for the petals and dust them with red and ruby petal dusts. The stamens are brown-tipped, as described for the orange flower above.

Moth orchid

There are many species of moth orchid (*Phalaenopsis*) and many more hybridised forms. The flower illustrated here is based on one that I have growing at home and that flowers very regularly. This is a difficult flower to make look realistic as it is quite flat looking. Most people crave the need to make the very flat, pure white moth orchids but I much prefer the hybridised, unusually coloured and spotted forms.

MATERIALS

White and yellow flowerpaste
26-gauge white wire
Fresh egg white
Sunflower, plum, African violet, daffodil, vine, white and foliage petal dusts
Isopropyl alcohol
White floristry tape

EQUIPMENT

Non-stick rolling pin
Scalpel
Moth orchid lip cutters (TT28, 25)
Non-stick board
Celstick or smooth ceramic tool
Scissors
Fine-nose pliers
Tweezers
Dusting brushes
Fine paintbrush
Ball tool

THROAT/LIP (LABELLUM)

1 Roll out some white flowerpaste, leaving a thick ridge for the wire. Cut out the labellum shape using the throat template on p 140 and a scalpel. Otherwise use one of the two sizes of moth orchid lip cutters to cut out the shape – the shape can vary a little between a just-opened and a fully opened orchid. Insert a 26-gauge white wire into the length of the thick ridge – this is quite a fragile shape so it is important that the wire passes through the narrow section of the shape.

2 Place the shape onto the non-stick board, elongate and broaden the two rounded side sections using a rolling action with the celstick or smooth ceramic tool to make them more oval in shape. Next, soften the edge of the whole shape and hollow out the two oval side sections. Pinch the length of the petal down the centre slightly back on itself to create a gentle ridge. The tip of the labellum may be left very pointed or trimmed into less of a point using scissors. In some moth orchids it can be fairly blunt.

3 Use fine-nose pliers to bend the wire and create a small hook at the base of the shape. Twist the hook slightly to tighten it. Next, attach a small cone-shaped piece of white flowerpaste over the hook to represent the column. Hollow out the underside by positioning the rounded end of the smooth ceramic tool under the shape and pressing the top of the column against it, creating a hollowed-out shape to the underside and a slight ridge to the upper surface. Curve the whole length of the labellum into the required curved shape.

4 To create the yellow ridged platform at the centre of the throat, simply form a small ball of yellow flowerpaste into a teardrop shape. Divide the broad end using the back of a scalpel blade or with tweezers to create a heart shape profile. Pinch the edges of the shape to thin them slightly. Trim the point off the base of the heart and attach at the heart of the throat/labellum petal with a small amount of fresh egg white. Leave to dry.

5 This step is optional, depending on the type of moth orchid you are making. There are often two fine strands at the very tip of the labellum that form a moustache shape. Roll these from white flowerpaste and attach to the tip of the labellum using fresh egg white or a tacky mixture of egg white and flowerpaste. In some varieties, the moustache curls and curves forwards at the tip, and in others it bends and curls backwards.

6 Carefully dust the raised platform and around its base onto the petal using sunflower petal dust. Dust the edges and base of the lip as required – here I have used a mixture of plum and African violet petal dusts and added fine detail spots using this colour mix diluted with isopropyl alcohol.

WINGS/ARMS (LATERAL PETALS)

7 Roll out some white flowerpaste, leaving a thick ridge for the wire. Cut out the petal shape using the wing template on p 140 and cut around it with a scalpel. Insert a moistened 26-gauge white wire into the thick ridge of the petal so that it supports a third to half the length of the petal. Pinch the base of the petal down onto the wire to neaten it and secure it in place. Soften the edge with a ball tool.

8 Place the petal into the wide petal veiner from the moth orchid veiner set. Press firmly to texture the surface. Remove from the veiner and pinch slightly at the base and the tip to create a little movement in the petal. Repeat to make a second petal – a mirror image of the first.

HEAD (DORSAL SEPAL)

9 Roll out some white flowerpaste leaving a thick ridge and cut out the sepal shape using a sharp scalpel and the head template on p 140. Insert a 26-gauge white wire into the central ridge to support about half the length. Soften the edge of the sepal using the ball tool. Next, place the sepal into the narrow veiner from the moth orchid set. Pinch the sepal at the base and at the tip, and then allow to dry, curved gently backwards – sometimes the tip curves forwards too.

LEGS (LATERAL SEPALS)

10 Repeat the method described for the dorsal sepal in step 9, using the more curved lateral sepal template on p 140. To create the second lateral sepal, flip the template over prior to cutting with the scalpel so that you create a left and a right sepal shape.

ASSEMBLY AND COLOURING

11 It is best to assemble the petals and sepals while they are still on the pliable side as this will allow you to curve and form them into a more relaxed shape, thereby creating a more realistic end result. Use half-width white floristry tape to tape the two wing petals onto either side of the labellum petal. Next, add the dorsal sepal tightly behind the wings to fill the gap that they have created. Finally, add and tape the lateral sepals (legs) behind the wings to fill in and complete the flower shape. Reshape the petals if needed.

12 Dust the petals and sepals with a light mixture of daffodil, vine green and white petal dusts, working from the base of each shape fading towards the edges and then dusting from the edge towards the centre. Don't forget to dust the backs too.

13 Add spotted detail using a mixture of African violet, plum and white petal dusts diluted with isopropyl alcohol. Use a dry mixture of these colours to catch the edges of the petals and sepals. Use a mixture of vine green and foliage to add a tinge of colour at the back of the flower where the petals and sepals join the main stem.

14 Allow the flower to dry and then hold over the steam from a just-boiled kettle, or if you are worried about the heat, try using a clothes steamer instead.

Vincent orchid

This pretty orchid is based on the *Isochilus* orchid. However, when making this in class I decided that the curved formation reminded me of the headbands that cake designer Kerry Vincent wears – and so I have nicknamed this the Vincent orchid!

COLUMN AND LIP (LABELLUM)

1 Cut a short length of 33-gauge white wire. Attach a tiny ball of pink flowerpaste to the end and work it down the wire leaving it slightly bulbous at the tip. Hollow out the underside using the rounded end of the celstick or smooth ceramic tool. Curve and leave to dry.

2 To make the lip, attach another piece of pink flowerpaste to a 33-gauge white wire and work the paste to create a fine tapered petal. Flatten it and vein with the stargazer B petal veiner. Pinch and curve the shape and then tape it onto the base of the column with quarter-width nile green floristry tape.

WING/LATERAL PETALS AND LATERAL SEPALS

3 The two wing petals are made as for the lip/labellum described above. Tape them onto the side of the column using quarter-width nile green floristry tape. These three petals form the framework on which the outer three sepals are added. These three are unwired but form the same shape as the petals. Attach to the orchid using fresh egg white. Curl back the tips of the petals and sepals. The flower looks almost like a bluebell in shape.

4 The buds are long, slender pieces of pink flowerpaste worked onto the end of a 30- or 28-gauge white wire. Divide into three to represent the outer sepals.

5 Tape the buds and flowers onto a 24-gauge white wire with nile green floristry tape to form a curved stem. Start with the smallest buds, gradually increasing in size and then add the flowers. Dust with plum and African violet petal dusts.

LEAVES

6 These are made almost like ruscus leaves. Blend a teardrop piece of holly/ivy flowerpaste onto a 30-, 28- or 26-gauge white wire and form it into a fine point. Flatten and vein using the stargazer B petal veiner. Pinch from the base to the tip. Repeat to make numerous leaves. Dust with foliage and vine petal dusts. Add tinges of aubergine to the edges. Spray lightly with edible spray varnish. Tape onto the flowering stem using half-width nile green floristry tape, starting with the smallest leaves and graduating in size down the stem. Curve the stem as you work.

MATERIALS
33-, 30-, 28-, 26- and 24-gauge white wires
Pink and holly/ivy flowerpaste
Nile green floristry tape
Fresh egg white
Plum, African violet, foliage, vine and aubergine petal dusts
Edible spray varnish

EQUIPMENT
Wire cutters
Celstick or smooth ceramic tool (HP)
Stargazer B petal veiner
Dusting brushes

Oxalis

There are about 800 oxalis species that are native in various forms throughout most of the world with a particular diverse group in Argentina, Brazil, Mexico and South Africa. The plant illustrated here is based on a plant that was posted to me by a very kind sugarcrafter. The plant is mostly grown for its very decorative foliage, which has the fascinating ability to open in daylight and close as the light diminishes.

MATERIALS

Pale pink, pale green and white flowerpaste

Fresh egg white

Plum, African violet, foliage, aubergine, vine, sunflower and white petal dusts

Edible spray varnish

White floristry tape

Fine white stamens

33-gauge white wire

Hi-tack non-toxic craft glue

EQUIPMENT

Non-stick rolling pin

Heart-shaped leaf cutter set (optional)

Plain-edge cutting wheel

Fine scissors

Large ball tool

Dusting brushes

Non-stick board

Stargazer B petal veiner (SKGI)

Cocktail stick

Scalpel

LEAVES

1 The leaves vary in the depth of colour so you will need to make some leaves with pale pink flowerpaste and others with pale green flowerpaste. Roll out some pale pink or pale green flowerpaste very thinly, leaving a fine ridge for the wire. Cut out the leaf shape using one of the sizes of heart-shaped leaf cutters or with the plain-edge cutting wheel and the template on p 140.

2 Insert a wire moistened with fresh egg white into the fine pointed end of the heart – the gauge will depend on the size of the leaf you are making. Next, use fine scissors to trim off the two curves of the heart shape to create a more angular leaf shape.

3

Soften the edge of the leaf using the large ball tool, which will help to thin the edge too. Use the small wheel of the plain-edge cutting wheel to add a faint central vein and several side veins to the leaf. Pinch the leaf from behind to accentuate the central vein. Repeat to make another two leaves of the same size.

COLOURING AND ASSEMBLY

4

Dust the base of each leaf, fading to the centre with plum petal dust. Add a light dusting of African violet over the top. Next, add a border of foliage green followed by a dense colouring to the edge with aubergine and a touch of plum. The smaller leaves tend to be more green in colour and less aubergine. Allow to dry, then gently steam or spray lightly with edible spray varnish.

5

Tape the leaves into their sets of three using quarter-width white floristry tape. Dust the stem with plum petal dust and a touch of foliage.

FLOWERS

6

Glue ten short fine white stamens to the end of a 33-gauge white wire using a small amount of non-toxic craft glue. Leave to dry and then dust the base with vine petal dust and the tips with sunflower petal dust.

7

Insert a 33-gauge white wire into the pointed base of a teardrop-shaped piece of white flowerpaste. Smooth the shape and remove any excess. Flatten it against the non-stick board using the flat side of the stargazer B petal veiner. Next, soften the edges with the ball tool and then texture using the double-sided stargazer B petal veiner.

8

Pinch the petal to create a central vein and then curl the edges slightly using a cocktail stick. Repeat to make five petals.

9

Tape the petals around the stamens using quarter-width white floristry tape. It is good if they are still pliable as this allows you to reshape and curl the petals as desired.

10

Dust the edges of the petals with a light mixture of plum, African violet and white petal dusts. Add a light tinge of vine mixed with foliage at the base of the flower to represent the calyx. Or if you have the time and patience, cut five fine sepals of pale green flowerpaste using the scalpel and attach them to the base of the flower. Dust the stem very lightly with a tinge of the flower colour and a little of the pale green colours used on the calyx.

Caper

It is the unopened flower buds that most people are familiar with – gathered and pickled in wine vinegar for cooking purposes. The fruit too is used in the same way, and even the foliage of the plant can be used pickled in salads. The plant originates from the Mediterranean area and has been introduced and grown widely in other warm territories. The beautiful flowers are very short-lived, lasting not even a day.

MATERIALS

Pale green cold porcelain (p 14–5)
33-, 28-, 26- and 22-gauge white wires
Vine, plum, African violet, white, foliage, aubergine and forest petal dusts
Seed-head stamens
Hi-tack non-toxic craft glue
White and pale green flowerpaste
Fresh egg white
Nile green floristry tape
Edible spray varnish

EQUIPMENT

Plain-edge cutting wheel
Dusting brushes
Scissors
Tweezers
Non-stick rolling pin
Rose petal or gardenia petal cutters
Large ball tool
Cupped Christmas rose petal veiner (SKGI)
Stargazer B petal veiner
Ceramic silk veining tool
Non-stick board
Fine-nose pliers
Briar rose leaf veiner (SKGI)

PISTIL

1 It is best to make the pistil with cold porcelain as this enables the stamens to be glued onto it with non-toxic craft glue. Roll a small ball of pale green cold porcelain and insert a 28-gauge white wire into it. Form the ball into a cone shape and then quickly work the base of the cone down the wire to form a long, fine pistil. Smooth the length between your palms. Divide the tip into four sections using the plain-edge cutting wheel. Curve the pistil slightly. Dust lightly with vine green and then add a tinge of aubergine onto the pointed tip.

STAMENS

2 The number of stamens can vary. It is best to assemble and glue small groups together and gradually add them to the pistil until the desired effect is achieved. Take groups of five to 10 stamens, line up the tips and glue one end with a small amount of non-toxic craft glue – try not to add too much as this will slow down the drying time and cut down the bulk.

3 Trim off the glued ends of the stamens, apply a little more glue and attach at the base of the pistil so that it protrudes higher than the stamen tips. Hold each bunch to the count of ten to hold them in place. Allow to dry and then open up the stamens using a pair of tweezers to pull and give the odd curl here and there.

4 Dust the base of the stamens with a mixture of plum and African violet. There are some varieties that have pure white stamens and others with green-tinged stamens.

PETALS

5 Roll out some well-kneaded white flowerpaste thinly, leaving a thick ridge for the wire. Cut out the petal shape using a rose petal cutter or a gardenia petal cutter – the shape can vary between varieties. Insert a 28-gauge white wire moistened with fresh egg white into the base of the thick ridge to support about a third of the length.

6 Soften the edge of the petal using the large ball tool and then texture using the double-sided cupped Christmas rose or stargazer B petal veiner. Remove from the veiner and cup the petal slightly. Sometimes the edges of the petals are slightly frilled – this can be achieved by rolling the edges with the ceramic silk veining tool. Repeat to make four petals.

COLOURING AND ASSEMBLY

7 Mix together African violet, plum and white petal dusts. Brush the colour from the base of each petal, fading a little at the edges. There are varieties with pure white petals, white petals tinged with green and pale pink too.

8 Tape the four petals evenly around the base of the stamens using quarter-width nile green floristry tape. Some varieties look as if they have only three petals but this is because they are almost fused together at the base.

CALYX

9 Cut short lengths of 33-gauge white wire. Insert a wire into a small teardrop-shaped piece of pale green flowerpaste. Place the shape against the non-stick board and flatten it using the flat side of one of the double-sided veiners. Next, hollow it out using the ball tool. Repeat to make four sepals – these may be of the same size or sometimes two large and two smaller sepals. Dust with foliage and vine petal dusts. Tinge with aubergine.

10 Tape the sepals onto the back of the flower using half-width nile green floristry tape. Dust the sepals with a mixture of white, vine and foliage petal dusts. Catch the edges with aubergine petal dust.

BUDS

11 These are the wonderful creatures we mostly buy pickled in wine vinegar – for years I was led to believe that they were the fruit of the nasturtium – however, these too can be pickled and used in the same way. These need to vary in size down the stem. Use 33- through to 28-gauge white wire, depending on the size you are working on. Bend a hook in the end of the wire. Form a small rounded cone shape and insert the hook moistened with fresh egg white into the base. Pinch a sharp point at the tip. Divide the surface into four to represent the outer sepals. Pinch a subtle ridge on each sepal.

12 Tape over the stem with quarter-width nile green floristry tape. Dust with various green petal dusts. The smaller buds tend to be a brighter green and benefit from a dusting of vine and foliage. The larger buds need more foliage and a touch of forest green too. All need a tinge of aubergine on the tips and a light dusting of white. Spray lightly with edible spray varnish.

FRUIT

13 These are much larger than the buds. Use 26-gauge white wire hooked in one end. Roll a ball of pale green flowerpaste and insert the wire into it. Work the ball into a slight point and then work the base of the shape down onto the wire to create a slender neck. Use the plain-edge cutting wheel to make a series of fine lines down the length of the shape. Dust with a mixture of foliage, white and forest green petal dusts. Tinge with aubergine. Spray lightly with edible spray varnish.

LEAVES

14 Use the rose petal cutters in various sizes for the foliage. Roll out some pale green flowerpaste, leaving a thick ridge for the wire. Cut out the leaf shape using one of the sizes of rose petal cutters. Position the cutter so that the point of the rose petal shape becomes the pointed tip of the leaf.

15 Insert a 28- or 26-gauge wire into the thick ridge to support about half the length of the leaf. Pinch the base of the leaf down onto the wire to create a more tapered appearance.

16 Soften the edge of the leaf and then texture using the double-sided briar rose leaf veiner. Pinch the leaf to accentuate the central vein. Repeat to make numerous leaves of various sizes.

17 Dust in layers with foliage, forest and white petal dusts. Tinge the base and the edges with aubergine. Tape over each leaf stem with quarter-width nile green floristry tape. Spray lightly with edible spray varnish.

18 Start taping the smallest leaves onto a 22-gauge white wire with half-width nile green floristry tape, alternating their position down the stem. Gradually increase the leaf size as you work down the stem. Introduce the buds at the same point that the leaves appear, increasing these in size too. Next, add the flowers again partnered with a single leaf.

19 Tape together other trailing stems using only the caper fruit and foliage. The buds and flowers are not usually on the same stems as the more mature fruiting parts of the plant.

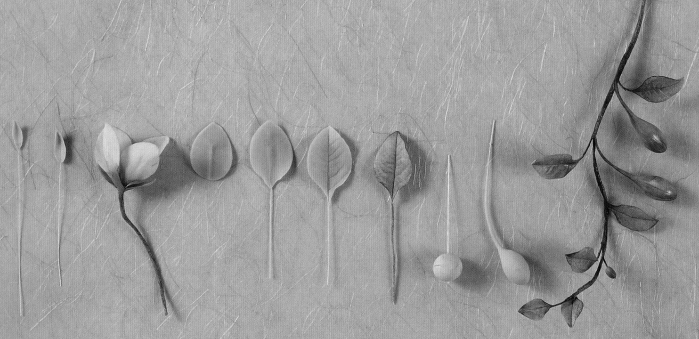

Old-fashioned rose

The centre of this rose is a little tricky to make but with a bit of patience and practice the results can be most effective. I love the depth of colour that some of these old-fashioned roses have, but of course you might prefer to use more delicate colouring.

INNER PETALS

1 Roll out some pale pink flowerpaste, leaving a thick ridge for the wire. Cut out a small rose petal shape using the smallest cutter from the rose petal cutter set and then insert a 26-gauge white wire moistened with fresh egg white into the thick ridge. Vein and thin out the petal using the ceramic silk veining tool to roll over the surface. Soften the edge with the ball tool.

2 Next, curl the petal into a spiral shape using a tiny amount of fresh egg white to hold it in place. Leave to dry. Repeat to make four more of these spiralled petals.

3 Roll out some more pale pink flowerpaste and cut out more petals using the same size cutter, plus the next size up in the set. Vein and soften as before.

4 Attach three or four petals around each of the wired spiralled petals using fresh egg white. Curl the edges a little as you add each petal.

5 Dust the petals heavily with a mixture of aubergine, plum and African violet. Dust the back of the petals with white petal dust.

6 Tape the five sections together using half-width nile green floristry tape. Leave to dry.

OUTER PETALS

7 Roll out some more pale pink flowerpaste, leaving a thick ridge for the wire. Insert a 26-gauge white wire moistened with fresh egg white into the thick ridge to support about half the length of the petal. Soften the edge of the petal and then vein using the rose petal veiner.

8 Hollow out the centre of the petal using the ball tool. Curl back the edges of the petal and leave to firm up slightly in a kitchen paper ring former. Repeat to make the required number of petals – usually about eight to 10. The size can vary a little too.

COLOURING

9 Dust the upper surface heavily with the same aubergine/plum/African violet mixture used earlier. Dust the back of each petal with white petal dust and introduce a little of the dark mixture to the edges too. A light glow of white mixed with vine green and daffodil can help to lighten the rose a little.

ASSEMBLY

10 Tape the outer petals around the inner curled petals using half-width nile green floristry tape. Curl the edges of the petals if they are still pliable. Allow to dry and then steam the flower lightly. Re-dust if a velvety effect is desired.

CALYX

11 Cut five lengths of 30-gauge white wire. Work a ball of pale green flowerpaste onto the wire, creating a long tapered carrot shape. Place the shape against the non-stick board and flatten using the flat side of one of the double-sided veiners. If the shape looks distorted, simply trim it into shape with scissors.

12 Place the flattened shape onto a foam pad or the palm of your hand, and soften and hollow out the length using the ball tool. Pinch the sepal from the base to the tip. Cut fine 'hairs' into the edge of the sepal using curved scissors. Repeat to make five sepals.

I tend to leave one sepal without hairs – although remember there are some varieties of rose that have no hairs to their calyces at all.

13 Dust each sepal on the outer surface with a mixture of foliage and forest petal dusts. Add tinges of aubergine mixed with plum or ruby petal dusts. Use the same brush used for the green mixture and dust lightly on the inner surface of each sepal with white petal dust. Lightly glaze the back of each sepal with edible spray varnish.

14 Tape the five sepals to the base of the rose, positioning a sepal over a join. Add a ball of pale green flowerpaste for the ovary and pinch and squeeze it into a neat shape. Dust the ovary to match the colouring of the sepal.

15 Alternatively, the calyx can be cut out in one piece using the rose calyx cutter. To do this, roll a ball of pale green flowerpaste and form it into a cone shape. Pinch the cone into a hat shape using your fingers and thumbs, leaving a rose hip shape at the centre to represent the ovary. Place the shape against the non-stick board and use a celstick or ceramic silk veining tool to roll out the brim of the 'hat'. Place the cutter over the paste with the rose hip/ovary shape at the centre and cut out the calyx shape. Remove the shape from the cutter and elongate each sepal using the ceramic silk veining tool or celstick. Hollow out the centre of each sepal using the ball tool and then add snipped hairy bits, as in step 12. Moisten the centre of the calyx and thread onto the back of the rose so that a sepal hides a join in the outer petals.

LEAVES

16 Roll out some pale green flowerpaste, leaving a thick ridge for the wire (a grooved board can speed up this process greatly). Cut out the leaves using the rose leaf cutters. You will find that the black rose leaf set does not allow for very thick leaves – these tend to stick in the cutter. Insert a moistened 26-, 28- or 30-gauge white wire into the leaf, depending on its size.

17 Soften the edge of the leaf and vein using the large briar rose leaf veiner. Pinch from behind the leaf to accentuate the central vein and give more movement to the leaf. Repeat to make leaves of various sizes. Tape over a little of each wire stem with quarter-width nile green floristry tape. Tape the leaves into sets of three or five, starting with the largest leaf and two medium-size leaves, one on either side. Finally, add the two smaller leaves at the base.

18 Dust the edges with aubergine and plum or ruby mixed together. Use this colour on the upper stems too. Dust the upper surface of the leaf in layers lightly with forest and heavier with foliage and vine petal dusts. Dust the backs with white petal dust using the brush used for the greens. Spray with edible spray varnish.

ROSE BUDS

19 These can be made following the instructions on page 73 (steps 1 to 5). You will need to keep the rose cone centre fairly small and use one of the smaller rose petal cutters from the rose petal set.

Degarmoara orchid

The Degarmoara orchid has actually been created by cross-hybridising three orchid genus from South America: the Brassia, Miltonia and Odontoglossum orchids. In fact, the cutter set I use for this orchid is used to create another cross-hybrid, the Miltassia orchid. It is always good to know that one set of cutters can be used for other projects too! This is another of the orchids that I bought at the early morning flower market in Brazil a few years ago. I love using this style of spidery orchid and the range of colours that these three species of orchid provide. They are fairly easy to make and add an unusual delicate yet exotic touch to floral sprays.

MATERIALS

33-, 26-, 24-, 22- and 20-gauge white wire
White and mid-green flowerpaste
Cornflour bag (p 11)
Nile green floristry tape
Vine, white, daffodil, plum, sunflower,
aubergine, ruby, foliage and forest petal dusts
Isopropyl alcohol
Fresh egg white
Edible spray varnish

EQUIPMENT

Scissors or wire cutters
Ceramic silk veining tool (HP)
Miltassia orchid cutters (TT878-880)
Metal ball tool
Stargazer B petal veiner (SKGI)
Dresden tool
Non-stick board
Fine-nose tweezers
Non-stick rolling pin
Foam pad
Dusting brushes
Fine paintbrush
Plain-edge cutting wheel
Large tulip leaf veiner (SKGI)

COLUMN

1 Cut a short length of 33-gauge white wire. Roll a tiny ball of white flowerpaste and then form it into a cone shape. Insert the wire into the pointed end of the teardrop. Work the paste down the wire slightly to create a more slender shape. Place the wired cone against the rounded end of the ceramic silk veining tool and press against it to hollow out the underside of the column. Use your finger and thumb to pinch and press against the tool, which will in turn create a slight ridge down the back of the column. Leave to dry.

LIP/THROAT (LABELLUM)

2 Squash the lip/labellum cutter from the miltassia orchid set into a more slender shape. Roll out some well-kneaded white flowerpaste, leaving a thick ridge for the wire. Cut out the labellum petal using the cutter.

3 Insert a moistened 26-gauge white wire into the thick ridge of the petal. Soften the edges using the metal ball tool to take away the cut edge effect.

4 Dust the surface of the petal lightly with cornflour and then place into the double-sided stargazer B petal veiner and press firmly to texture the surface of the petal.

5 Use the broad end of the Dresden tool to work the edges of the petal against the non-stick board and then go back over the edge to frill with the ceramic silk veining tool.

6 Use fine-nose tweezers to pinch two fine ridges at the base (wire end) of the petal to create a platform. Pinch the petal down the centre and then push and pinch back a waistline shape on the petal. Allow to firm up a little before taping onto the column with half-width nile green floristry tape. Make sure the column is facing with the hollowed side down towards the surface of the petal.

WINGS/ARMS (LATERAL PETALS)

7 Roll out some white flowerpaste, leaving a fine ridge for the wire. Cut out the wing petal shape using the wing template on p 140. Insert a moistened 26-gauge white wire into the thick ridge so that it supports about a third to half the length of the petal. Soften the edge using the metal ball tool, working half on the paste and half on your hand or foam pad.

8 Texture the petal using the stargazer B petal veiner. Pinch from the base to the tip and curve the petal backwards slightly. Repeat to make a second wing petal, which should create a mirror image of the first.

HEAD (DORSAL SEPAL)

9 Roll out some white flowerpaste and cut out the dorsal shape using the longer cutter in the set or the head template on p 140.

10 Insert a moistened 26-gauge white wire into the thick ridge to support about half the length of the petal. Soften the edge and vein as for the wing petals. Curve the dorsal backwards and allow to firm up slightly.

LEGS (LATERAL SEPALS)

11 Repeat as for the dorsal sepal to create a mirror image of the lateral sepals. Curve the legs and allow to dry a little.

ASSEMBLY AND COLOURING

12 Tape the two lateral petals onto either side of the labellum and column using half-width nile green floristry tape. Next, add the dorsal sepal followed by the lateral sepals. If the flowerpaste is still pliable at this stage, it will give you a chance to create more interesting curves and a realistic finish.

13 Dust the petals with a light mixture of vine green, white and a touch of daffodil petal dusts mixed together. Start dusting at the base of each petal and fade out towards to tip. Tinge the edges of the petals with plum petal dust. Use sunflower petal dust to colour the two ridges at the base of the labellum.

14 Dilute a mixture of aubergine, ruby and plum petal dusts with isopropyl alcohol and paint detail spots onto the labellum and outer petals. There are some varieties with no spots if you are feeling nervous about painting. Dust the back of the flower at the base of each petal/sepal with foliage petal dust.

BUDS

15 Roll a ball of well-kneaded white flowerpaste and form it into an elongated teardrop shape. Insert a hooked 26-gauge white moistened with fresh egg white into the broader end of the teardrop to support about half the length of the bud.

16 Use the plain-edge cutting wheel to divide the bud into three sections. Curve the bud slightly. Repeat to make buds of varying sizes. Dust as for the flower.

17 Tape the buds, starting with the smallest, onto a 20-gauge white wire with half-width nile green floristry tape.

LEAVES

18 Roll out a long length of mid-green flowerpaste, leaving a thick ridge for the wire. Cut out the long strap-like leaf shape using the plain-edge cutting wheel. Insert a 24-or 22-gauge white wire into the ridge, depending on the size of the leaf.

19 Soften the edge and vein using the double-sided large tulip leaf veiner. Pinch from the base to the tip. Dry to create a graceful curve. Repeat to make another leaf slightly shorter in length.

20 Dust in layers with forest and foliage green. Tinge the edges with aubergine. Spray lightly with edible spray varnish.

Clematis

There are around 200 species of clematis distributed across the world and many more hybrid forms. The flowers can have four to eight outer petal-like segments and many of the hybrid varieties are double in form. The size, colour and form of this family are vast, providing the cake decorator with a good variety to work with.

MATERIALS

Seed-head and hammerhead stamens
Hi-tack non-toxic craft glue
28-, 26-, 24- and 22-gauge white wires
Vine, white, aubergine, plum, foliage and African violet petal dusts
Isopropyl alcohol
Edible spray varnish
White and mid-green flowerpaste
Fresh egg white
Nile green floristry tape

EQUIPMENT

Scissors
Fine angled tweezers
Dusting brushes
Non-stick rolling pin
Clematis petal cutter (optional)
Plain-edge cutting wheel
Large ball tool
Asiatic lily or clematis petal veiner (Aldaval)
Ceramic silk veining tool (HP)
Fine-nose pliers
Simple leaf cutters (TT225-232)
Clematis Montana leaf veiners (SKGI)

STAMENS

1 Take a few small groups of seed-head stamens and apply non-toxic craft glue at the centre of each group to bond and hold them together. Flatten the glue as you apply it and try not to add too much as it will take much longer to dry. Cut each group in half using scissors and trim off the tips and some excess from the un-glued ends. Next, apply a little more glue to one of the groups and wrap around the end of a 22-gauge white wire, pinching it firmly onto the wire to create a good, strong bond. Leave to dry and then continue to add the other small groups in the same way to create a tight, compact centre. Allow to dry and trim shorter again if necessary.

2 The threads of the hammerhead stamens are a little thicker, making them ideal for the longer outer stamens. Glue a few stamens at a time and repeat the above trimming process prior to attaching these longer stamens around the tighter group on the wire. Once the glue has dried, trim the stamens and curve these outer stamens using fine angled tweezers.

3 Dust the stamens lightly with a mixture of vine green and white petal dusts. The colouring does vary between varieties of clematis. I have painted the tips of the stamens with aubergine and plum mixed with isopropyl alcohol. Leave to dry and then set the colour onto the stamens using a light spray of edible spray varnish.

PETALS

4 Roll out some well-kneaded white flowerpaste, leaving a thick ridge for the wire. Cut out the petal shape using the clematis petal cutter or refer to the clematis petal template on p 140 and use a plain-edge cutting wheel to cut around the shape.

5 Insert a 26-gauge white wire moistened with fresh egg white into about a third of the length of the thick ridge of the petal. Work the base of the petal down onto the wire to give a strong join. Soften the edge of the petal gently with the large ball tool.

6 Place the petal in the double-sided Asiatic lily or clematis petal veiner and press firmly to texture the petal. Remove from the veiner and rest the petal against your index finger which will act as a platform while you frill at intervals around the edges of the petal with the ceramic silk veining tool.

7 Pinch the petal from the base to the tip to accentuate the central veins and curve the tip slightly. Allow to firm up a little before colouring. Repeat to make eight petals.

COLOURING AND ASSEMBLY

8 Dust the base and tip of each petal lightly with a mixture of vine green and white petal dusts. Add a strip of this colour down the back of the petals. Over-dust the back at the base slightly with foliage green. Mix together African violet and plum petal dusts with a touch of white and dust a stripe down the centre of the upper surface of each petal. Add a stronger stripe of colour over the top if you wish.

9 Tape the petals around the stamens using half-width nile green floristry tape. If the petals are still pliable at this stage it will help you reshape and give a more relaxed feel to the finished flower.

BUDS

10 Bend a hook in a 24- or 22-gauge white wire using fine-nose pliers – the gauge will depend on how big the bud is to be. Form a cone of well-kneaded white flowerpaste and insert the hooked wire moistened with fresh egg white into the broad end. Divide the surface of the bud into eight sections using the plain-edge cutting wheel or a knife. Pinch a central ridge down the length of each using fine angled tweezers (preferably without teeth!). Twist the bud slightly. Dust the base of the bud to match the flower with a tinge of vine green at the tip. The smaller buds should have more green to their make-up. The odd tinge of aubergine helps too.

LEAVES

11 These come in sets of three – generally one large and two slightly smaller leaves, one on either side. I prefer the toothed edge of the clematis Montana leaves and so I create my own hybrid forms combining them with the larger showy clematis types. Roll out some mid-green flowerpaste, leaving a thick ridge for the wire.

12 Cut out the leaf shape using one of the simple leaf cutters. Insert a 28-, 26- or 24-gauge white wire into the thick ridge of the leaf to support about half its length. Soften the edge of the leaf and vein using one of the clematis Montana leaf veiners. Pinch from the base gently to the tip to accentuate the central vein. Repeat to make leaves in sets of three.

13 Dust in layers with foliage and vine green petal dusts. Tinge the edges with aubergine. Glaze lightly with edible spray varnish. Tape the leaves into their sets of three using half-width nile green floristry tape. Dust the taped stems on the upper surface with aubergine petal dust.

Siam tulip

Often known as **Curcuma**, this unusual ornamental flower is part of the ginger family related to the section that provides turmeric. Its pretty sounding common name could be misleading as it is not related to the tulip family at all! The ornate petal-like segments are actually modified bracts which can be white, pink or mauve in colour – the true flowers are small and hidden in the green bracts at the base. I have used the small flowers in bud form only as they are much simpler to make.

BUDS

1 Form a small cone of white flowerpaste and insert a hooked 26-gauge white wire moistened with fresh egg white into the broad base. Thin down the base onto the wire to create a slightly longer, slender shape. Pinch three petals from the tip of the bud and twist around to tighten the shape. Dust with African violet and plum petal dusts.

BRACTS

2 Roll out some white flowerpaste, leaving a thick ridge for the wire. Cut out the bract shape using one of the sizes of sage leaf cutters or the templates on p 140 and the plain-edge cutting wheel. Insert a 28- or 26-gauge white wire into the ridge, depending on the size of the bract. Soften the edge and then vein using the double-sided stargazer B petal veiner.

3 Next, pinch the shape from the base to the tip and hollow out the centre of the bract using your thumb. Repeat to make several bracts in varying sizes – the number varies quite a bit. Allow the bracts to firm up a little before assembling them into the flower head.

4 You might prefer to dust the bracts prior to assembly – I prefer to assemble and dust the head as a whole piece. Start by taping the smaller bracts onto the end of a 20-gauge white wire using half-width nile green floristry tape. Continue adding the bracts spiralling around the stem and increasing the bract size as you work.

5 Next, roll out some pale green flowerpaste and cut out a series of rose petal shapes. Soften the edge, vein and hollow as for the large bracts. Add these bracts at the base of the wired bracts, allowing them to retain a cupped shape. Curl back their edges as you add them and also start to tape in the flower buds encased by a single bract.

6 Dust the green bracts with vine, moss and foliage petal dusts. Tinge the tips of the white bracts gently with vine green and over dust with smaller amounts of moss and foliage. Mix African violet, plum and white petal dusts together and add a flush of colour to each of the white bracts from the base fading towards the tip. Add the odd tinge of aubergine mixed with African violet to the green bract. Steam to set the colour.

MATERIALS

White and pale green flowerpaste
28-, 26-, and 20-gauge white wires
Fresh egg white
African violet, plum, vine, moss, foliage, white and aubergine petal dusts
Nile green floristry tape

EQUIPMENT

Fine-nose pliers
Dusting brushes
Non-stick rolling pin
Sage leaf cutter set (TT852-855) (optional)
Plain-edge cutting wheel
Stargazer B petal veiner (SKGI)
Rose petal cutters (TT)

Hazelnuts

Hazels (*Corylus*) are a genus of deciduous trees and large shrubs that are native to the temperate northern hemisphere. The nuts of all hazels are edible, with the common hazel being the most extensively grown, followed by the Filbert.

MATERIALS

Pale green and cream flowerpaste

26- and 24-gauge white wires

Fresh egg white

Foliage, vine, terracotta, tangerine, nutkin, champagne and cream petal dusts

Edible spray varnish

Nile green floristry tape

EQUIPMENT

Non-stick rolling pin

Hazel leaf veiner set (SKGI)

Plain-edge cutting wheel

Metal ball tool

Rose petal cutters (optional)

Non-stick board

Dresden tool

Dusting brushes

Scriber or needle

Fine-nose pliers

Scalpel

Six-petal pointed blossom cutters (OP)

LEAVES

1 Roll out some well-kneaded pale green flowerpaste, leaving a thick ridge for the wire – do not roll the flowerpaste too fine as the hazel leaf veiners are quite heavily veined and will cut through the paste if it is too fine. Insert a 26-gauge white wire moistened with fresh egg white into about half the length of the thick ridge (use 24-gauge for larger leaves).

2 Place the wired flowerpaste into one of the double-sided hazel leaf veiners, lining up the central vein with the wire. Press the two sides together firmly to texture the leaf. Remove from the veiner and trim the excess paste away using the plain-edge cutting wheel. Soften the edge with the metal ball tool. To speed up the process a little, you might prefer to use rose petal cutters to cut out the basic leaf shape. This does tend to make the leaves a little too regular but will save you a little time.

3 Place the front side of the leaf down against the non-stick board and work the edges with the broad end of the Dresden tool to create a more serrated, ragged finish. Next, pinch the leaf down the centre to accentuate the central vein. Allow to firm up a little before dusting with petal dusts.

COLOURING

4 Dust the leaves as required. The smaller new growth is a fresher green so use layers of foliage and vine green. For the larger autumnal foliage, use terracotta, tangerine and nutkin on the edges. Dust foliage and vine green from the base towards the edges. Leave to dry and then spray lightly with edible spray varnish. Add insect nibbles and weather damage to the edges by attacking the leaves with a scriber, needle or wire that has been heated until red hot (using a cigarette lighter or tea-light). Tape over the wire with half-width nile green floristry tape.

NUTS

5 Roll a ball of well-kneaded cream-coloured flowerpaste. Form it into more of an oval shape and then insert a hooked 24-gauge white wire moistened with fresh egg white into the base.

6 Pinch the upper edge on either side of the nut to create a slight ridge on either side, keeping the base still rounded. Pinch the tip into a sharper point.

7 Use a scalpel, scriber or plain-edge cutting wheel to make a series of lines down the sides of the nuts. Dust with champagne and cream petal dusts. Add a slight tinge of vine green and foliage mixed with champagne petal dusts. Spray lightly with edible spray varnish.

HUSK

8 Roll out some pale green flowerpaste not too thinly. Cut out a shape using the six-petal pointed blossom cutter. Elongate the central petal on either side of the shape so that they are longer than the other petals which also need increasing only very slightly in length.

9 Use the broad end of the Dresden tool to work the edges of each section to thin it and create a more ragged husk-like finish. Attach onto the back of the nut with the shortest sections at the side of the nut. Curl back the edges using your fingers.

10 Dust the husk with foliage and vine green. Add tinges of cream and nutkin.

11 Repeat to make the nuts in pairs or sets of three. Snuggle them tightly together before they have a chance to dry.

Brassada orchid

This spider-like orchid is from South America and is actually a cultivated cross-hybrid between a Brassia orchid and an Ada orchid. I love the long curly petals that these flowers have. These orchids tend to be mostly orange or yellow in colour but I see no reason why the colour scheme could not be given a touch of artistic licence!

MATERIALS

White/cream and green flowerpaste
33-, 28-, 26-, 24-, 22- and 20-gauge white wires
Cyclamen liquid food colour
Fresh egg white
Nile green floristry tape
Sunflower, daffodil, aubergine, tangerine, coral, foliage and vine petal dusts
Edible spray varnish

EQUIPMENT

Ceramic silk veining tool (HP)
Scalpel
Fine paintbrush
Non-stick rolling pin
Small alstromeria petal cutter (TT438)
Dresden tool
Stargazer B veiner (SKGI)
Fine angled tweezers
Non-stick board
Scissors
Dusting brushes
Plain-edge cutting wheel
Large tulip leaf veiner (SKGI)

COLUMN

1 Attach a small ball of white/cream flowerpaste onto the end of a 33-gauge white wire. Work the paste down the wire to form a teardrop shape. Place the shape against the rounded end of the ceramic silk veining tool to hollow out the underside. Curve the shape. Add another cap if desired by adding a tiny ball of flowerpaste onto the tip of the column. Split the ball in half using a scalpel. Paint spots on the underside with cyclamen liquid food colour.

LIP (LABELLUM)

2 Roll out some well-kneaded white/cream flowerpaste, leaving a thicker ridge at the centre for the wire. Cut out the lip shape using the alstromeria petal cutter. Insert a 28-gauge white wire moistened with fresh egg white into the ridge. Broaden the base of the petal to create a flap on either side using the broad end of the Dresden tool. Soften the edges of the petal and vein using the double-sided Stargazer B veiner.

3 Frill the edges of the lip using the ceramic silk veining tool. Pinch back the base of the lip and pinch the tip into a sharp point.

4 Pinch two ridges at the base of the petal using fine angled tweezers to create the characteristic raised platform. Allow to dry a little before colouring.

WING/LATERAL PETALS

5 There are two wing petals. Work a small ball of white/cream flowerpaste onto a length of 28-gauge white wire. Form the shape into a long pointed petal shape. Place against the non-stick board and flatten the shape using the flat side of the stargazer B veiner. Trim the edges if required using scissors. Vein using the Stargazer B veiner. Pinch the petal from the base to the tip to accentuate the central vein. Curve each petal back slightly so that they are a mirror image of each other.

DORSAL (HEAD) AND LATERAL (LEGS) SEPALS

6 These are made in the same way as the wing petals but you need to make the legs much longer. Curve the dorsal petal back slightly and curl the tips of the leg petals before the flowerpaste has a chance to dry.

COLOURING/ASSEMBLY

7 Tape the column onto the labellum petal using half-width nile green floristry tape. Next add the two shorter outer petals (arms) and finally the outer three petals. If the flowerpaste is still pliable at this stage you can reshape it to create a more natural finish.

8 Dust the lip lightly with a mixture of sunflower and daffodil petal dusts. Paint spots onto the lip using cyclamen liquid food colour mixed with aubergine petal dust. Some Brassada orchids have raised spots on the throat while others have simple spotted markings.

9 Dust the outer petals and sepals with tangerine petal dust to create an intense colouring. Add a tinge of coral to the petal edges too. Paint spots at the base of each petal.

BUDS

10 These are long and slender. Add teardrop-shaped piece of white/cream flowerpaste onto a 26-gauge white wire. Work into a slender point. Divide into three using the plain-edge cutting wheel or scalpel. Curve into shape. Dust as for the flower.

ASSEMBLY

11 Tape the buds onto a 20-gauge white wire using half-width nile green floristry tape. Alternate the buds starting with the smallest and graduating the size as you work. Finally add the flowers. Dust the stem with foliage green. Add tinges of aubergine to the tips and the base of the buds.

LEAVES

12 Roll out some green flowerpaste, leaving a thick ridge for the wire. Use the plain-edge cutting wheel to cut out a freehand, not-too-slender leaf shape.

13 Insert a moistened 24- or 22-gauge white wire into about half the length of the leaf. The exact gauge will depend on the size of leaf you are making.

14 Place the leaf into the double-sided large tulip leaf veiner and press the two sides together firmly to texture the surface of the leaf. Remove the leaf from the veiner and carefully pinch it from the base to the tip to accentuate the central vein. Allow to dry in a slightly curved position.

15 Dust in layers with foliage green and vine green petal dusts. Catch the edges with aubergine. Allow to dry further and then glaze using edible spray varnish.

Chinese lantern

These ornamental forms of physalis are native to China, Korea and Japan, and are related to the popular Cape gooseberry, which is actually South American in origin but cultivated in South Africa and other parts of the world too for its edible fruits. The ornamental forms also produce an inedible fruit that is concealed inside the inflated and very decorative calyx, which turns orange as the stems mature. Florists often strip the leaves from the plant to make more of a feature of the lanterns – I personally prefer them with the foliage. There are instructions for the flowers too, although these are optional. When I started to demonstrate years ago it was these and the nasturtium that became my signature flowers!

MATERIALS

28-, 26-, 24-, 22- and 20-gauge white wires

White, pale green, orange and pale melon flowerpaste

Small white seed-head stamens

Hi-tack non-toxic craft glue

Daffodil, sunflower, white, vine, tangerine, coral, foliage and aubergine petal dusts

Fresh egg white

Clear alcohol (Cointreau or kirsch)

Piece of polystyrene

Edible spray varnish

Nile green floristry tape

EQUIPMENT

Fine-nose pliers

Scalpel or plain-edge cutting wheel

Dusting brushes

Celstick

Small rose calyx cutters (OP or TT)

Non-stick rolling pin

Physalis leaf veiners (SKGI)

Clematis leaf veiner (SKGI)

Fine paintbrush

Large rose calyx cutters (OP or TT244)

Non-stick board

Fine scissors

Angled tweezers

BUD

1 Insert a hooked 26-gauge white wire into the base of a teardrop-shaped piece of white flowerpaste. Thin down the neck slightly. Divide the tip into five using a scalpel or plain-edge cutting wheel.

FLOWER

2 Glue five short seed-head stamens to the end of a 26-gauge white wire using non-toxic craft glue. Add a sixth stamen with the tip cut off to represent the pistil. Leave to dry and then curl them slightly. Dust the tips with a mixture of daffodil, sunflower and white petal dusts. Dust the base with vine petal dust.

3 Form a teardrop-shaped piece of white flowerpaste and pinch the base to form a hat shape. Roll out the 'brim' of the hat using the celstick. Cut out the flower shape using one of the small rose calyx cutters.

4 Broaden each petal with the celstick, rolling either edge of each petal and leaving a thicker area at the centre of each. Open up the centre of the flower using the pointed end of the celstick. Pinch a central vein down each petal and then thread the stamens through the centre of the flower. Thin the back of the flower a little and remove any excess flowerpaste.

CALYX

5 Add a ball of pale green flowerpaste at the base of the flower and the bud. Roll out some pale green flowerpaste and cut out a small calyx shape using the same size cutter as used to make the flower. Roll each sepal and broaden them with a celstick. Vein each sepal using the small physalis leaf veiner or clematis leaf veiner. Thread onto the back of the ball of flowerpaste, so that the raised veins produced by the back of the leaf veiner are on show. Moisten the edges of each sepal with fresh egg white and carefully join them together around the back of the flower/leaf so that it looks like a small lantern shape. Leave to dry. Dust with vine green and catch the edges with a little tangerine petal dust. Paint fine spots using sunflower, daffodil and white petal dusts diluted with clear alcohol. Add tinges of vine to the tips of the bud and the petals.

'LANTERNS'

6 These can be made with orange-coloured flowerpaste or with a pale melon base dusted to the varying degrees of green through to bright orange. Form a large teardrop-shaped piece of flowerpaste and then pinch out the broad end to form a large hat shape. Roll out the paste around the centre – not too thinly at this stage.

7 Use a large rose calyx cutter to cut out the basic shape of the lantern. You will need a few sizes of cutter to create a variation in lantern size down the stem.

8 Next, place the shape flat against the non-stick board and broaden each sepal with the celstick, leaving a thick ridge running down the centre of each. This will create wider sepals and thin the paste too. Elongate the sepals slightly too.

9 Vein each sepal using the physalis or clematis leaf veiner, making sure that the raised veins on the back of the leaf are used to create the texture on the upper surface of each sepal.

10 Bend a hook in the end of a 22-gauge white wire. Heat the wire using a tea-light until it goes red hot. Quickly thread the wire through the solid centre of the shape, embedding the hot hook into the flowerpaste. This caramelises the sugar to form a good instant bond. Be very careful not to burn your fingers on the hot sugar!

11 Next, moisten the edges of each sepal with fresh egg white. At this stage it is often best to insert the other end of the wire into a piece of polystyrene to hold the shape and give you both hands free to join and squeeze the edges of each sepal together. I often find it best to join two pairs together and then join these together leaving the fifth sepal to simply slot in. Trim off any excess paste from the edges of the sepals using fine scissors.

12 Use angled tweezers to continue the ridged vein made by the veiner to the centre of the shape where the wire comes out. Leave to set for a little while, but not dry completely, before dusting.

13 Dust the lantern in layers of tangerine, a touch of coral, tinges of foliage green, and on some you can introduce tinges of aubergine. The smaller lanterns at the top of the stem will be more green in colour, with gradual introduction of the orange and coral. Allow to dry before spraying lightly with edible spray varnish.

LEAVES

14 The leaves occur singular and in pairs, and sometimes even in sets of three. I generally use one leaf to each bud, flower and lantern. Roll out some pale green flowerpaste, leaving a thick ridge for the wire. Press the flat side of the chosen size of physalis leaf veiner against the paste to leave an outline. Use the plain-edge cutting wheel to cut out the shape.

15 Insert a 28-, 26- or 24-gauge white wire into the leaf so that it supports about half the length of the leaf.

16 Soften the edge of the leaf and then place into the double-sided physalis leaf veiner to texture it. Remove from the veiner and pinch from the base to the tip to accentuate the central vein. Tape over each leaf stem with half-width nile green floristry tape.

17 Dust with vine green, foliage and tinges of aubergine. Spray lightly with edible spray varnish or steam the leaves to set the colour.

ASSEMBLY

18 Tape a few smaller leaves at the end of a 20-gauge white wire using half-width nile green floristry tape. Gradually introduce the buds accompanied by one or two leaves. Next, add the flowers, again with leaves at the same point and then finally use the smaller lanterns with their heads hanging downwards with foliage at the same point gradually working through to the larger, more mature, lanterns. Dust the stem with vine, foliage and tinges of aubergine petal dusts. Spray the stem lightly with edible spray varnish to seal the colour onto the stems. Bend the stem slightly to create a bit of movement.

Ilex berries

Ilex verticillata is a native holly from America and Canada. The plant loses its foliage during the autumn, allowing these glossy berries to shine brightly on naked stems. The berries can be yellow, orange or red, making them a very useful addition to autumn and winter displays.

MATERIALS

35-, 33-, 22-, 20- and 18-gauge white wires
Sunflower yellow flowerpaste
Fresh egg white
Sunflower, tangerine, foliage, aubergine and nutkin petal dusts
Edible spray varnish
Full glaze (p 12) (optional)
Brown floristry tape

EQUIPMENT

Wire cutters
Fine-nose pliers
Tea light
Flat dusting brushes

BERRIES

1 Cut 35- or 33-gauge white wire into five or six short lengths. Take five or six short wires at a time and line up the ends to then bend them all in one fail swoop using fine-nose pliers.

2 Using the tea light, burn the hooked end of the wires to leave them looking black.

3 Roll balls of sunflower yellow flowerpaste to make the berries. Moisten the hook with fresh egg white and pull through a single wire into each ball. Leave to firm up a little before the next stage.

4 Dust the berries to create the desired effect. Here, I have dusted in layers with sunflower and over-dusted with tangerine petal dusts. Allow to dry and then spray with edible spray varnish or dip into a full glaze. You might need a few layers of glaze to create very shiny berries. Allow to dry. Dust the short stems with foliage and aubergine petal dusts.

5 Tape over a short length of 22-gauge white wire with half-width brown floristry tape to create a twig effect. Tape the berries tightly onto the twig. To create a larger piece, tape several smaller twigs onto a 20- or 18-gauge white wire.

6 Dust the twigs carefully with nutkin petal dust. Be very careful not to catch the berries too much with this colour. Spray lightly again with edible spray varnish.

Acer

There are around 120 species of Acer throughout the northern hemisphere. The variety I have chosen to use in this book has leaves made up of three to seven finer individual leaves. The beautiful autumnal colouring of the foliage makes the Acer an ideal addition to the flower-maker's repertoire.

LEAVES

1 Cut short lengths of 33-, 30- or 28-gauge white wires. The gauge of wire will depend on the size of foliage you are planning to make.

2 Roll a ball of well-kneaded pale green flowerpaste. Wrap it around the wire at the length required and then work the paste to the tip to form it into a fine point. You will need to work firmly and quickly to create a smooth finish.

Next, place the coated wire between the fleshy part of your palms and smooth the whole shape.

3 Place the wired shape against the non-stick board and flatten it using the flat side of the large briar rose leaf veiner – a method that I commonly refer to as SPLAT! Remove the veiner and check to see that the shape is good – if it isn't, you will need to trim the edge using the plain-edge cutting wheel or small scissors.

4 Soften the edge of the leaf with the small ball tool and then texture using the double-sided large briar rose leaf veiner. Remove from the veiner and pinch from the base to the tip to accentuate the central vein. Curve accordingly. Repeat to make varying sizes of leaf.

5 Tape the leaves into 'hand' shapes using quarter-width nile green floristry tape – these groupings can be made up of three to nine sections. If the leaves are still pliable, then reshape them to create a more natural overall design.

MATERIALS

33-, 30-, 28-gauge white wires
Pale green flowerpaste
Nile green floristry tape
Sunflower, tangerine, coral, ruby, aubergine and foliage petal dusts
Edible spray varnish

EQUIPMENT

Wire cutters
Non-stick board
Large briar rose leaf veiner (SKGI)
Plain-edge cutting wheel or small scissors
Small ball tool
Dusting brushes

6 Dust the leaves in varying layers while the paste is still wet. Use sunflower, tangerine, coral, ruby and aubergine in turn until the desired depth of colour is achieved. Add tinges of foliage too if required. Allow to dry and then spray lightly with edible spray varnish.

Cucumis fruit

These decorative fruit belong to the *Cucurbitaceae* family that includes the more familiar pumpkin, marrow, melon, gherkin and gourd. They are great for autumnal and winter floral displays and because of their size fill a good space too. The foliage is mostly stripped away by florists to reveal the brightly coloured fruit.

MATERIALS

33-, 28-, 26- and 24-gauge white wires
Nile green floristry tape
Pale cream flowerpaste
Fresh egg white
Sunflower, tangerine, coral, red, ruby, foliage, vine and aubergine petal dusts
Isopropyl alcohol
Edible spray varnish

EQUIPMENT

Scissors
Plain-edge cutting wheel
Dusting brushes
Fine paintbrush

TENDRILS

1 Tape over lengths of 33-gauge white wire with quarter-width nile green floristry tape. Smooth over the tape by rubbing the sides of a pair of scissors against it. Curl and tangle the tendril to give plenty of movement. Repeat to make several tendrils.

FRUIT

2 Roll a ball of well-kneaded pale cream flowerpaste. Form it into an oval, almost egg shape. Insert a 28- or 26-gauge white wire moistened with fresh egg white into the fruit so that the wire protrudes through the end. Pinch the paste at the tip and at the base to secure it in place. Texture the surface slightly with lines created with the plain-edge cutting wheel. Repeat to make varying sizes of fruit.

COLOURING AND ASSEMBLY

3 Dust to varying degrees with sunflower, tangerine, coral, red and ruby petal dusts. Add tinges of foliage mixed with vine and also tinges of aubergine.

4 Dilute some of the foliage and vine petal dusts with isopropyl alcohol to paint very fine lines onto the surface.

5 Tape a tendril onto the end of a 24-gauge white wire with half-width nile green floristry tape. Start to add smaller fruit and graduate down the stem, adding tendrils at the same point as each fruit. Curl the stem as required. Dust it with foliage and aubergine petal dusts. Glaze the fruit with edible spray varnish.

Chincherinchee

I love the name of this South African flowering bulb.
I have chosen to use orange chincherinchees in this
book but there are also white and yellow forms.

OVARY AND STAMENS

1 Attach a small cone-shaped piece of green cold porcelain onto the end of a 33-gauge white wire so that the tip of the wire very slightly protrudes. Work the base of the cone into a more slender shape. Squeeze the sides of the ovary between two fingers and a thumb to create three sides. Mark a line on each side using the scalpel. Dust with a mixture of foliage and navy petal dusts. Using non-toxic craft glue, glue six short seed-head stamens around the ovary and leave to dry. Dust the tips of the stamens with sunflower petal dust.

PETALS

2 Work a ball of cream flowerpaste onto the end of a short length of 33-gauge white wire. Form it into a cigar shape slightly pointed at both ends. Place the shape on the non-stick board and flatten it using the back of the cupped Christmas rose petal veiner. Soften the edges and then texture using the veined side of the same veiner.

3 Cup and pinch the petal into shape. Repeat to make six petals. Tape the petals around the stamen centre using quarter-width nile green floristry tape. Dust the petals with tangerine and tinges of coral petal dusts.

BUDS

4 Insert a 22-gauge white wire into a slender teardrop piece of pale green flowerpaste. Smooth the sides between your palms. Use fine scissors to snip into the surface of the flowerpaste to create the bracts that form a scaled effect at the top of the stem.

5 Add small, wired cigar-shaped buds to the stem, adding a bract to each bud made by cutting a pointed shape from some pale green flowerpaste. Attach to the stem with fresh egg white. Dust the buds to match the flowers. Dust the green bracts with vine and foliage petal dusts. Add tinges of aubergine.

6 Tape the flowers onto the stem using half-width nile green floristry tape. Add a flowerpaste bract at the base of each of these flowers where the short flower stems meet the main stem. Dust the bracts as for the smaller bracts at the top of the stem. Dust the main stem with vine green and a touch of foliage green.

MATERIALS

Green cold porcelain (p 14–5)
33- and 22-gauge white wires
Foliage, navy, sunflower, tangerine, coral, vine and aubergine petal dusts
Hi-tack non-toxic craft glue
Seed-head stamens
Cream and pale green flowerpaste
Nile green floristry tape
Fresh egg white

EQUIPMENT

Scalpel
Dusting brushes
Non-stick board
Cupped Christmas rose petal veiner (SKGI)
Fine scissors

Fantasy butterflies

A few years ago my friend and very talented cake decorator John Quai Hoi introduced me to his wired sugar butterflies. I have been hooked on making them ever since! You might decide to copy the wing designs of real butterflies but I find them more fun made with a fantasy approach.

MATERIALS

35-, 33-, 28- and 26-gauge white wires
White flowerpaste
Fresh egg white
Seed-head stamens
Non-stick rolling pin
Cornflour bag (p 11)
White or nile green floristry tape
Vine, African violet, plum and aubergine petal dusts
Isopropyl alcohol
Hi-tack non-toxic craft glue (optional)
Non-toxic disco glitters (EA) (optional)

EQUIPMENT

Fine-nose pliers
Scalpel or plain-edge cutting wheel
Non-stick rolling pin
Butterfly cutters (Jem) or templates on p 140
Metal ball tool
Hibiscus petal veiner (SKGI) or anemone petal veiner (Aldval)
Dusting brushes
Fine paintbrushes

THE BODY

1 The body can be made as an all-in-one shape and divided into sections using a scalpel or you can make it as I do in three sections joined together. Using fine-nose pliers, bend a hook in the end of a 26-gauge white wire. Roll a ball of white flowerpaste for the centre of the body (thorax) and insert the wire moistened with fresh egg white into it. Pinch it firmly to secure the two together. Next, roll a smaller ball of white flowerpaste for the head and stick it onto one side of the body with fresh egg white. Divide this section in half using the scalpel or plain edge-cutting wheel to create two eyes. Form a carrot shape and attach at the other side of the body to represent the abdomen.

2 Curl a short length of 35- or 33-gauge white wire to represent the tongue (proboscis) and insert into the head area, through the body and into the tail – this should help to give more support to the whole shape.

3 Cut one seed-head stamen in half to give two lengths to represent the antennae. Trim both a little shorter if desired and insert one into each eye. Leave to dry.

WINGS

The butterfly cutters that I prefer contain the four wing sections in one plastic piece – it drives me nuts. So I have taken a large pair of scissors to my set and cut them in half – I find this much easier to deal with now!

4 Roll out some well-kneaded white flowerpaste, leaving a fine ridge for the wire. Cut out the larger wing section using the wing cutter. Carefully remove the shape from the cutter and insert a 28-gauge white wire moistened with fresh egg white into the thick ridge to support about half the length of the wing.

5 Soften the edge with the metal ball tool and then texture the wing using the double-sided hibiscus or anemone petal veiner. Dust the wing with cornflour prior to veining to prevent it sticking to the veiner and take care not to press too hard so that you don't cut through the paste.

6 Pinch the wing from the base to the tip to give a little movement. Repeat to make the opposite wing section plus the two smaller lower wings. Leave to firm a little before assembling and colouring.

ASSEMBLY AND COLOURING

7 Tape the larger forewings onto either side of the body using white or nile green floristry tape. Position and tape the smaller hind wings slightly behind the forewings.

8 As these are fantasy butterflies, you can colour them as you desire or even just leave them white. I have used layers of vine green at the base of the wings and a mixture of African violet and plum on the edges.

9 Dilute some aubergine petal dust with isopropyl alcohol and paint over the body, antennae and proboscis using a fine paintbrush. Add detail spots and catch the extreme tips with this diluted colour too. Allow to dry.

10 If you feel like a bit of glitz, then simply apply a thin layer of non-toxic craft glue to the tips of the wings and the antennae and dip into disco glitter – please note that although these glitters are non-toxic they are not a food item! Therefore I would only recommend that you use the glitter to decorate items that are not intended to be eaten.

CELEBRATION
CAKES

Boy's christening

An old-fashioned perambulator is the main feature of this charming christening cake. A patchwork approach embellished with pearlised dragées and gold stars creates a rather magical and whimsical aura to this cake design. Of course, the colour scheme can be altered to make it suitable for a girl too.

MATERIALS

20 cm (8 in) round fruitcake placed on a thin cake board of the same size
750 g (1½ lb) almond paste
1 kg (2 lb) white sugarpaste
Fine turquoise ribbon
Royal icing
Pearlised dragées
Broad turquoise ribbon
Pins or non-toxic craft glue stick (Pritt)
White flowerpaste
Clear alcohol (Cointreau or kirsch)
White vegetable fat
Mug and saucer
Cocoa butter, grated
Myrtle, white bridal satin, bluegrass, antique gold and classic gold petal dusts
Green sugar crystals
Gold edible star sprinkles

EQUIPMENT

30 cm (12 in) round thick cake drum
Small plain scalloped marzipan crimpers
Small stitchwork wheel (PME)
Non-stick rolling pin
Oval plaque cutters
Round plaque cutters in various sizes
Ruler
Sharp knife
Small fine-nose angled tweezers
Clay gun
Fine paintbrush and dusting brushes

FLOWERS

5 single chincherinchee flowers (p 95)

PREPARATION

1 Cover the cake as described on p 16. Cover the cake drum with white sugarpaste, then crimp the edge with the small plain scalloped marzipan crimpers. Transfer the cake on top of the cake drum. Next, add some stitch work lines onto the cake surface using the small stitchwork wheel to create a ground effect to position the pram on. Attach a fine band of turquoise ribbon around the base of the cake, using a dab of royal icing or softened sugarpaste to hold it in place at the back. Tie five tiny bows of fine turquoise ribbon and attach at intervals around the base of the cake. Embed a single pearlised dragée above each bow using a dab of royal icing to hold it in place. Secure a broad band of turquoise ribbon to the cake drum's edge using pins or non-toxic craft glue. Allow the cake to dry overnight before continuing with the design.

PATCHWORK PERAMBULATOR

2 Mix together equal amounts of white flowerpaste and sugarpaste to create a pliable modelling paste. Roll out the paste so that it is not too thin and cut out two oval shapes using one of the oval plaque cutters to represent the body of the pram and cut two smaller round shapes for the wheels. Use a ruler and a sharp knife to cut away the excess paste of each oval to create the desired depth of base and hood of the pram – refer to the template on p 141 to create the correct shaping. Use one of the smaller circle cutters to cut several crescent-shaped indents from the hood shape.

3 Moisten the back of each section of the pram with clear alcohol and attach onto the surface of the cake. Quickly use the small fine-nose angled tweezers to create the line/framework on the hood. Next, use the stitchwork wheel to add stitching lines to the hood and the base of the pram.

4 Use the same size circle cutter used for the wheels to remove two curved sections at the base of the pram to make way for the cut-out wheels. Attach the wheels onto the pram, removing a small crescent shape from one wheel to allow the second wheel to sit in place. Use the small circle cutter to make the centre of each wheel and the larger circle cutter to create the inner line of the tyres. Use a combination of the tweezers and stitchwork wheel to create the spokes.

5 To create the curly pram handles, soften a small amount of white flowerpaste with white vegetable fat and extrude it

through a small hole fitting in the clay gun. Attach to the pram, curling either end as you position them. Secure pearlised dragées into the curl of each end and also at the centre of both wheels – you might need a tiny dot of royal icing to hold them in place.

6 To complete the paintwork on the pram, melt some grated cocoa butter onto a dish above a mug filled with just-boiled water, and use myrtle, white bridal satin, bluegrass and both golds mixed together in turn to add detail and shading to the pram and the dragées around the base of the cake. Add a collection of green sugar crystals at the base of the pram using tiny dots of royal icing to secure them in place. Finally, position the individual chincherinchee flower heads around the base of the cake and sprinkle the tiny gold stars above the pram and around the cake drum at intervals.

18th birthday

A cake design suitable for a shoe-loving woman of any age! The feathered texture of the unusual nigella flowers complements the peacock feathers perfectly. The shoe, feathers and side design have been embossed into the sugarpaste coating while the paste was still soft and then painted over with melted coloured cocoa butter.

MATERIALS

25 cm (10 in) round rich fruitcake placed on a thin cake board of the same size

1.25 kg (2 lb 10 oz) white almond paste

2 kg (4½ lb) champagne sugarpaste

Tracing or greaseproof paper

Blue dragées

Mug and saucer

Cocoa butter, grated

White, plum, forest, foliage, vine, white bridal satin, cornflower and African violet petals dusts

Edible gold leaf-covered flowerpaste

Gold braid

Royal icing

Blue organza ribbon

Pins or non-toxic craft glue stick (Pritt)

Gold and pink paper-covered wires

Pink crimped wire

Assorted beads

EQUIPMENT

35 cm (14 in) round thick cake drum

Scriber or pen that has run dry

Plain-edge cutting wheel

Stitch effect wheel (PME)

Small circle cutter set

No.4, No.3 and No.2 piping tubes

Paintbrushes

FLOWERS

2 nigella flowers, plus foliage (p 22–3)

EMBOSSING

1 Cover the cake and cake drum as described on p 16–7. Trace the shoe template on p 142 onto tracing or greaseproof paper and then scribe it onto the surface of the cake using a scriber or a pen that has run dry. Mark the main lines of the feathers using the plain-edge cutting wheel, and the finer lines using the stitch effect wheel. Add the eye markings to the feathers using a series of small circle cutters. Add embossed dots to the sole of the shoe and in amongst the feathers using various sizes of piping tubes. Embed a single blue dragée into the centre of each peacock eye detail.

2 Emboss the side design onto the cake using a series of circle cutters followed by dotted detail and flower embossing with No.4, No.3 and No.2 piping tubes. Again, attach a single dragée into the centre of the flower design. At this stage you might prefer to leave the sugarpaste to dry before painting in the details. I was impatient when I created this cake and so decided to paint directly onto the wet sugarpaste!

COLOURED COCOA PAINTING

3 Melt some grated cocoa butter onto a dish above a mug filled with just-boiled water. Mix in small amounts of petal dusts as they are required to create the painting medium. I have used white and plum for the main colour of the shoe. Allow each layer to set before darkening the mixture to add shaded and defined areas to the design. Paint in the feather lines and trailing vine around the shoe using the various greens mixed with white bridal satin petal dust. Paint over the blue dragées with cornflower blue, African violet and white bridal satin mixed together.

4 Add some dried broken pieces of gold leaf-covered flowerpaste to the heal and front of the shoe (see p 19 for more information).

5 Paint over the embossed side designs to pick up the same colouring as used in the shoe design. The cocoa-painted designs will dry but be careful not to store the cake in a hot room or touch the design too heavily as the design can melt again.

6 Attach a band of gold braid around the base of the cake using a dab of royal icing or softened sugarpaste to hold it in place at the back. Secure two bands of blue organza ribbon to the cake drum's edge using pins or non-toxic craft glue.

7 Tape two corsages using the nigella flowers, gold and pink paper-covered wires and pink crimped wire with beads. Position one spray on top of the cake and the other at the base.

21 today!

This effective tie design could be adapted for several masculine occasions – perhaps incorporating a hobby design onto the tie too, such as painted rugby balls, musical notes, etc. The pretty blue sun orchids help to soften the design, creating a very special centrepiece.

MATERIALS

25 cm (10 in) elliptical rich fruitcake placed on a thin cake board of the same size
1.25 kg (2 lb 10 oz) white almond paste
1.25 kg (2 lb 10 oz) white sugarpaste
Floral blue ribbon
Royal icing
Blue ribbon
Non-toxic craft glue stick (Pritt)
Pale lavender-coloured flowerpaste
Edible silver leaf
Clear alcohol (Cointreau or kirsch)
African violet, deep purple, white bridal satin, foliage and vine petal dusts
Blue sugar crystals

EQUIPMENT

35 cm (14 in) elliptical Perspex board
Non-stick rolling pin
Key cutter (Jem)
No.6 and No.3 piping tubes
Number cutters (FMM)
Scalpel or plain-edge cutting wheel
Large ball tool
Dusting brushes
Fine paintbrushes

FLOWERS

7 blue sun orchids, plus buds (p 28)
6 Japense ferns (p 27)

1 Cover the cake as described on p 16. Place the coated cake onto the Perspex board. Attach a band of floral blue ribbon around the base of the cake using a dab of royal icing or softened sugarpaste to hold it in place at the back. Secure a band of blue ribbon to the edge of the Perpex board using non-toxic craft glue.

21 AND KEY

2 Roll out some pale lavender-coloured flowerpaste thinly and attach it to a sheet of edible silver leaf (see p 19 for more information). Cut out the key shape using the key cutter and then remove three holes from the decorative end using a No.6 piping tube. Keep these cut-out shapes to add as a decoration on the tie, removing a hole in the centre of each with the No.3 piping tube. Cut out more of these circles from the excess flowerpaste.

3 Cut out numbers 2 and 1 from the silver leaf-covered flowerpaste using the number cutters. The paste will stick in the shape – these can be removed by tapping the cutter firmly against the work surface. Attach the numbers and the key onto the coated cake using clear alcohol.

THE TIE

4 Roll out some pale lavender coloured-flowerpaste not too thinly and cut out a tie shape using a scalpel or plain-edge cutting wheel. Soften the edges of the paste with the large ball tool, trying not to give a frill to the edges. Fold over the top section of the tie to create a 'knot'.

5 Dust the tie, concentrating on the edges, with a mixture of African violet, deep purple and white bridal satin petal dusts. Over-dust with more white bridal satin. Moisten the back of the tie sections with clear alcohol and place onto the cake, trying to give a little movement to the edges of the long section.

6 Decorate the tie using the small cut-out silver circles. Add painted detail at the centre of each circle, using a fine paintbrush and African violet and deep purple petal dusts mixed together with clear alcohol. Add detail to the leaves and stems using foliage, vine and white bridal satin mixed together. Add extra texture to the tie by painting very fine lines with white bridal satin diluted with clear alcohol. Attach blue sugar crystals onto the tie to complete the design.

7 Paint trailing vines around the key and numerals using the clear alcohol and petal dusts mix used to colour the design on the tie. Dust lightly around the tie to soften the background with white bridal satin mixed with foliage and vine petal dusts.

8 Arrange the sun orchids and fern to create a large display at the back of the cake. Add a shorter stem of orchids and fern at the base of the cake to balance the design.

Valentine sweet hearts

Gold hearts encrusted with red, purple and pink sugar crystals have been used on this Valentine's cake to complement the boldness of the red rose and sweet violet spray.

1 Cover the cake and cake drum as described on p 16–7. Attach a thin band of red velvet ribbon around the base of the cake, using a dab of royal icing or softened sugarpaste to hold it in place at the back. Secure the broader red velvet ribbon to the cake drum's edge using pins or non-toxic craft glue.

SUGAR-ENCRUSTED HEARTS

2 Quickly sprinkle some coloured sugar crystals over some gold leaf-covered flowerpaste (see p 19 for more information) and then roll over them with the non-stick rolling pin to bond them onto the surface. Cut out several heart shapes in various sizes. Attach with clear alcohol to the top edge of the cake and around the cake drum too.

3 Melt some grated cocoa butter onto a dish above a mug filled with just-boiled water. Mix in some African violet, vine and white petal dusts and paint some fine dotted floral designs between the hearts using a fine paintbrush.

BEETLEWEED LEAVES

4 Use the basic leaf-making principle to create these leaves from pale green flowerpaste. Cut out the shape using the beetleweed cutters. Insert a 26- or 24-gauge white wire moistened with fresh egg white into the leaf. Work the edge using the broad end of the Dresden tool to create a more irregular effect to the serrated edge that the cutter gives. Soften the leaf and then vein using the galex leaf veiner. Pinch to accentuate the central vein. Dust in layers of ruby, aubergine and foliage. Allow to dry before spraying with edible spray varnish.

SPRAY ASSEMBLY

5 Using the rose as the focal point, tape together the flowers and the foliage using half-width nile green floristry tape. Insert the posy pick into the cake and then position the handle of the spray into it to complete the cake design.

Mothering Sunday

This charming cake uses the very simple technique of sugar-pressed flowers as its focal decoration. This style of flower-making is ideal for a novice cake decorator or as a fairly quick design for a cake.

MATERIALS

15 cm (6 in) round rich fruitcake placed on a thin cake board of the same size

450 g (12 oz) white almond paste

450 g (12 oz) champagne sugarpaste

Thin lavender ribbon

Royal icing

Foliage, white, vine, African violet, plum, aubergine, white bridal satin, daffodil, sunflower and plum petal dusts

Clear alcohol (Cointreau or kirsch)

Green, white and pale yellow flowerpaste

Black paste food colour

EQUIPMENT

23 cm (9 in) round decorative plate

Fine paintbrush

Non-stick board

Non-stick rolling pin

Set of 3 Australian fern cutters

Australian daisy leaf cutter

Plain-edge cutting wheel or Dresden tool

Dusting brushes

Daisy paper punch

Scalpel

Scriber

Rose petal cutters or pansy set (TT)

Ceramic silk veining tool

Cocktail stick

Clear sugarpaste smoother

SIDE DESIGN

1 Cover the cake as described on p 16. Place the coated cake onto the decorative plate. Attach a band of thin lavender ribbon around the base of the cake, using a dab or royal icing or softened sugarpaste to hold it in place. Tie and attach four small bows evenly spaced onto it.

2 Paint the design onto the sides of the cake using clear alcohol to dilute some foliage, white and vine petal dusts for the foliage section of the design, and then add the dotted flowers using a mixture of white, African violet and plum.

PRESSED LEAVES AND FLOWERS

3 The leaves are very simple to create – on a non-stick board, simply roll some green flowerpaste very thinly and cut out assorted shapes using a selection of fine cutters. Here I have used the Australian fern cutters and a fine daisy leaf cutter. Soften the edges, trying to keep each shape quite flat. Add very light central veins using the plain-edge cutting wheel or the fine end of the Dresden tool. Dust the fern leaves with foliage petal dust. Add tinges of African violet and aubergine to the edges. Dust the fine daisy leaves with foliage and over-dust with white bridal satin. Attach to the top of the cake using clear alcohol painted onto the

back of each leaf. It is often best to position the items onto the cake without moistening so that you can create a good display prior to the final attachment. The daisies were cut out from thinly rolled white flowerpaste and a daisy paper punch. The petals were then split using a scalpel blade. The centre of the flowers is a simple ball of pale yellow flowerpaste flattened and textured using the scriber.

4 The pansies can be cut out using a set of pansy cutters which is basically made up from one heart-shaped lip cutter and two sizes of rose petal cutters, or you can use two sizes of rose petal cutters to cut out three large and two smaller petals from some thinly rolled white flowerpaste. Remove a 'V' shape cut from one of the larger petals to create the heart-shaped lip shape. Vein and broaden the lip petal using the ceramic silk veining tool, working on each half of the petal at a time to control an even shape. Frill and thin the edges further with a cocktail stick. Vein and frill the remaining large petals and the two small petals.

5 Overlap the two large petals, moistening to join them and then place the two smaller petals on top at each side followed by the large heart-shaped petal.

Use the broad end of the Dresden tool to embed the lip petal into the centre of the flower. Roll a fine strand of white flowerpaste and fold into a 'V' shape. Moisten and add to the centre of the flower to create the characteristic white eyebrow that the flowers have. Next, 'press' the flower using a clear sugarpaste smoother (or something similar); this will flatten the frills giving quite a realistic finish.

6 Dust the lip of the flower from the centre with a mixture of daffodil and sunflower petal dusts. Use a mixture of African violet and plum for the larger petals and the edges of the other petals. Add fine lines to the lip and the small side petals using a fine paintbrush and black paste food colour.

7 Attach the pansies and daisy flowers over the fern and daisy leaf shapes. Use the smoother again to add extra 'pressing' if required. Add fine-painted leaves and dotted flowers on the top of the cake as described for the side design.

Father's Day

Although this cake was intended as a Father's Day cake for a keen gardener, it could also be used as a retirement cake or even as a birthday cake for a vegetarian or gardener!

MATERIALS

20 cm (8 in) elliptical fruitcake placed on a thin cake board of the same size

750 g (1 lb 10 oz) white almond paste

1 kg (2 lb) champagne sugarpaste

Pale green flowerpaste

Fresh egg white

Vine, foliage, moss, aubergine and white bridal satin petal dusts

Edible spray varnish

Clear alcohol (Cointreau or kirsch)

Brown velvet ribbon

Pins or non-toxic craft glue stick (Pritt)

Pink paper-covered wire

Food-grade plastic posy pick

EQUIPMENT

30 cm (12 in) elliptical cake drum

Non-stick rolling pin

Plain-edge cutting wheel

Ball tool

Fine scissors

Dusting brushes

No.4, No.3 and No.2 piping tubes

Paintbrushes

FLOWERS AND VEGETABLES

5 peapods (see step 1)

13 radishes (p 38–9)

8 asparagus (p 37)

2 stems of potato vine (p 40–1)

Cover the cake and cake drum as described on p 16–7.

PEAPODS

1 These are great fun to make! I actually made them on a train journey to London for one of the photo shoots for this book! I had lots of strange looks from fellow passengers as I rolled the peas into shape. Several of them went rolling around the carriage – peas that is! Use pale green flowerpaste and roll lots of balls in slightly varying sizes. Leave to set a little.

2 Next, roll out some more pale green flowerpaste and cut out a pointed leaf shape using the plain-edge cutting wheel. Soften the edge with the ball tool and add indents on either side of the shape using the small end of the ball tool. Pinch a vein down the centre to form the pod. Moisten with fresh egg white and attach the peas to one side of the pod and then carefully fold over the other half to encase them. Pinch and shape the pod accordingly. Leave to set until firm enough to add a small five-sepal calyx (made from a cone of pale green flowerpaste hollowed in the centre and snipped into five sections using fine scissors. Pinch and thin each sepal between your fingers and then attach to the top of the peapod. Leave to dry. Dust the whole thing in layers of vine, foliage and moss petal

dusts. Tinge with aubergine. Allow to dry completely before spraying lightly with edible spray varnish.

EMBOSSED PEAPODS

3 These need to be embossed into the freshly coated cake and drum using the No.4, No.3 and No.2 piping tubes to create the pea shapes. Next, add the peapod outline using the plain-edge cutting wheel. Dust the embossed shapes with a light mixture of white bridal satin, vine and foliage. Dilute a little of the colour with some clear alcohol to paint tendrils and define detail on the peas and the pod.

4 Secure a band of brown velvet ribbon to the edge of the cake drum using pins or non-toxic craft glue. Tie a bunch of radishes together with a length of pink paper-covered wire to display on top of the cake. Insert a slender posy pick behind the radish to hold the upright stem of potato vine. Tuck three stems of asparagus underneath the radishes. Assemble an informal display of peapods, radishes, asparagus and potato vine around the base of the cake.

Engagement

I have used a painted heart design on this pretty heart-shaped cake to symbolise an engagement, echoed in the curled, almost ring-like, shapes of the beaded wires used in the floral spray along with roses – the flower most often used to demonstrate a couple's love for one other.

MATERIALS

20 cm (8 in) heart-shaped rich fruitcake placed on a thin cake board of the same size

750 g (1 lb 10 oz) white almond paste

1 kg (2 lb) white sugarpaste

Narrow pale pink ribbon

Royal icing

Broad pale pink ribbon

Pins or non-toxic craft glue stick (Pritt)

Tracing or greaseproof paper

Mug and saucer

Cocoa butter, grated

Foliage, vine, white, plum and aubergine petal dusts

Nile green floristry tape

Lilac beaded wires

Food-grade plastic posy pick

EQUIPMENT

30 cm (12 in) heart-shaped cake drum

Fine scriber or pen that has run dry

Paintbrushes

Wire cutters

Fine-nose pliers

FLOWERS

1 pink rose and 1 rosebud, plus foliage (p 32–5)

3 pachyveria succulents (p 29)

3 single white chincherinchee flowers (p 95)

7 dianthus flowers, plus buds and foliage (p 30–1)

3 green beetleweed leaves (p 106)

1 stem of Japanese painted fern (p 27)

PREPARATION

1 Cover the cake and cake drum as described on p 16–7. Attach a band of narrow pale pink ribbon around the base of the cake, using a dab of royal icing or softened sugarpaste to hold it in place at the back. Secure the broader pale pink ribbon to the cake drum's edge using pins or non-toxic craft glue. Leave the cake to dry for a few days before painting the design onto the surface.

CAKE TOP DESIGN

2 Trace the dianthus flower template on p 141 onto tracing or greaseproof paper and scribe it onto the top of the cake using a fine scriber or a pen that has run dry.

3 Melt some grated cocoa butter onto a dish above a mug filled with just-boiled water. Mix in small amounts of petal dust to create the painting medium. Paint the design in layers, allowing each section to set before adding shading and detail. Add some painted dots at the opposite side of the cake, curving up onto the surface of the cake, alternating between a mixture of foliage, vine and white, and plum mixed with white to soften the colours. Add a dark detail at the centre of the dianthus flowers using aubergine petal dust mixed with melted cocoa butter.

SPRAY

4 Use the large rose as the focal point and, using half-width nile green floristry tape, tape the other flowers and foliage around it to create a tapered shape. Bind the flowers together to form a handle for the spray.

5 Cut lengths of lilac beaded wires, turning over each cut end with fine-nose pliers to prevent the beads from escaping. Curl the wires into shape and tape them into the spray to soften the edges of the shape. Insert a posy pick into the side of the cake. Bend the handle of the spray and insert it into the posy pick. Curl and bend the beaded wires to create an attractive shape to fit with the curves of the cake.

Rose and orchid wedding

Brush-embroidered royal-iced roses are used to complement the beautiful sprays of pink and orange roses and orchids on this two-tiered wedding cake.

MATERIALS

25.5 cm (10 in) leaf shape rich fruitcake placed on a thin cake board cut to the same size

15 cm (6 in) oval rich fruitcake placed on a thin cake board of the same size

1.4 kg (3 lb) white almond paste

1.4 kg (3 lb) pale pink sugarpaste

Pink organza ribbon

Royal icing

Piping gel (optional)

Rose and gooseberry paste food colours

Clear alcohol (Cointreau or kirsch)

Plum, white, tangerine, sunflower, daffodil, vine and foliage petal dusts

Nile green floristry tape

Food-grade plastic posy pick

EQUIPMENT

35 cm (14 in) oval Perspex board

Straight-edged sugarpaste smoother

Fine scriber or pen that has run dry

2 piping bags fitted with No.1 tubes

Assorted paintbrushes

Silver candleholder

FLOWERS

3 large orange roses (p 32–5)

10 pink half roses (p 32–5)

8 brassada orchids (p 86–8)

7 rose hips (p 36)

12 sprigs of ilex berries (p 92)

5 sprigs of pink brunia (p 42)

15 red beetleweed leaves (p 106)

1 Cover the cakes as described on p 16. Place the leaf shape sugarpaste-coated cake on top of the Perspex board and use the straight-edged sugarpaste smoother to create a good bond between the cake and the board. Attach a band of pink organza ribbon around the base of both cakes, using a dab of royal icing or softened sugarpaste to hold it in place. Leave to dry for a few days before executing the brush embroidery.

BRUSH EMBROIDERY DESIGN

2 This can be traced onto the surface of the coated cakes using the template on p 141 and a fine scriber or a pen that has run dry. Or you might prefer to pipe freestyle to complete the design.

3 You might prefer to add a teaspoon of piping gel to the royal icing to slow down the drying process: use 1 teaspoon of piping gel to 4 tablespoons of royal icing. Colour some of the royal icing pale pink and some to a pale green using rose and gooseberry paste food colours respectively. Fit two piping bags with No.1 tubes and fill with the coloured icings.

4 Using the piping bag filled with pink royal icing, start to pipe over the scribed lines of the rose petals. Apply quite a bit of pressure to give you enough royal icing to brush into a petal shape. Use a brush large enough to fit the design and dampen the bristles slightly with water – don't use too much water as this will swamp the design and dissolve the sugar; if you use too little water, the icing will end up with a dry finish. Brush the petal from the edge, leaving a raised border, and form petal veining as you work. Continue piping and brushing the petals until the rose is complete, following the direction of the veins in the petal.

5 Next, pipe in the rose leaves using the piping bag filled with pale green royal icing. Once again, use a damp paintbrush to create a veining process on each leaf. Leave to dry before painting.

6 Use clear alcohol to dilute the plum petal dust with a touch of white and then the tangerine mixed with plum to colour the rose petals. Add diluted sunflower and daffodil at the base of each petal. Use vine and foliage with a touch of white diluted to colour the leaves. Use a fine paintbrush to add fine painted vine leaves in between each of the roses.

7 Place the sugarpaste-coated oval cake on top of the candleholder and tilt the leaf shape cake at the base. Use the large orange roses as the focal point for each of the three sprays and gradually add the half roses, brassada orchids, rose hips, ilex berries and sprigs of pink brunia to complete the sprays, using nile green floristry tape to hold the sprays together. Next, tape in the red beetleweed leaves around the flowers to frame the sprays. Insert the large spray into a posy pick in the top tier. Rest the medium-size spray in the indent at the back of the bottom tier and position the small spray at the front.

Ruby birthday

This colourful two-tiered cake was designed for a 40th birthday celebration – with the butterfly symbolising just how quickly the years fly by! The bold use of a ruby-coloured peony also makes the design suitable for a ruby anniversary cake or even for a small wedding cake – with the addition of another symbolic butterfly of course!

MATERIALS

Non-toxic glue stick (Pritt) or double-sided stick tape

15-cm (6-in) and 20-cm (8-in) round rich fruitcakes placed on thin cake boards of the same size

1 kg (2 lb) white almond paste

1.4 kg (3 lb) white sugarpaste coloured with bluegrass paste food colour

Fine aqua satin ribbon

Royal icing

Broad colourful floral ribbon

Pins or non-toxic craft glue stick (Pritt)

Tracing or greaseproof paper

Mug and saucer

Cocoa butter, grated

White, plum, aubergine, foliage, vine, bluegrass and sunflower petal dusts

Blue, pink and yellow paper-covered wires

Nile green floristry tape

Large food-grade plastic posy pick

EQUIPMENT

Two 30-cm (12-in) round cake drums

Scriber or a pen that has run dry

Fine paintbrushes

FLOWERS

1 peony, plus foliage (p 43–5)

5 sprigs of pink brunia (p 42)

7 trails of hearts entangled (p 26)

1 fantasy butterfly (p 96–7)

PREPARATION

1 Double up the cake drums and stick them together using non-toxic craft glue or doubled-sided sticky tape. Cover the cakes and cake drum as described on p 16–7.

2 Next, position the larger cake on top of the cake drum and then place the smaller cake on top of it. Attach a band of fine aqua satin ribbon around the base of the cakes, using a dab of royal icing or softened sugarpaste to hold it in place. Secure a band of broad floral ribbon to the doubled-up cake drums' edge using pins or non-toxic craft glue.

COCOA PAINTING

3 The side design can be painted freehand or you may prefer to trace the floral design from the template on p 142 onto tracing or greaseproof paper and then scribe the design onto the side of the cakes using a scriber or a pen that has run dry. Melt some grated cocoa butter onto a dish above a mug filled with just-boiled water. Be careful not to apply too much heat as this will make the medium too runny to paint with; equally, if the heat is not sufficient it will be too thick to paint with.

4 Add small amounts of petal dust in turn to execute the floral design using fine paintbrushes. The addition of a touch of white petal dust will create a more opaque painting medium. Use plum to colour the peony flower and buds. Add depth and finer details by adding a touch of aubergine to the plum. Use foliage and vine petal dusts mixed together to paint the foliage, adding more foliage to define the leaf shapes and to add shading. Use bluegrass to paint dotted flowers and flowing lines through the design. Finally, add sunflower yellow petals into the design to soften the edges. Allow the design to dry and if desired, etch away some fine detail lines in the petal and leaf formations.

5 Use the peony as the focal point, surrounded by its foliage and sprigs of brunia. Add trails of coloured paper-covered wires and hearts entangled foliage, holding the flowers together with nile green floristry tape. Add a single wired fantasy butterfly to the bouquet and then insert into a large posy pick pushed into the top tier. Re-arrange any of the elements as required.

Golden days

Golden sugar dragées add a touch of glamour and embellishment to this beautiful celebration cake that could also be suitable as an alternative centrepiece for a golden wedding anniversary party.

MATERIALS

25 cm (10 in) leaf-shaped rich fruitcake placed on a thin cake board of the same size

1.4 kg (3 lb) white almond paste

2 kg (4½ lb) lilac sugarpaste

Fine lilac ribbon

Lilac royal icing

Green leaf-like ribbon

Broad lilac velvet ribbon

Pins or non-toxic craft glue stick (Pritt)

Sugar pearl dragées in varying sizes

Small amount of white flowerpaste

Antique gold, pearl, African violet, white, plum and antique gold petal dusts

Clear alcohol (Cointreau or kirsch)

Nile green floristry tape

Lilac, gold and green paper-covered wire

Food-grade plastic posy pick

EQUIPMENT

35 cm (14 in) leaf-shaped thick cake drum

Piping bag fitted with a No.1 piping tube

Fine paintbrush

FLOWERS

1 brassolaeliacattleya orchid (p 48–51)

5 sprigs of lilac (p 55)

1 Siam tulip (p 83)

9 pink dianthus, plus buds (p 30–1)

14 sprigs of French lavender (p 56–7)

2 lilac half roses and one bud (p 32–5)

3 pachyveria succulents (p 29)

3 stems of trailing caper flowers, plus fruit (p 70–2)

1 Cover the cake and cake drum as described on p 16–7. Attach a band of fine lilac ribbon around the base of the cake, using a dab of royal icing or softened sugarpaste to hold it in place. Attach the green leaf-like ribbon slightly above the finer ribbon. Secure a band of broad lilac velvet ribbon to the cake drum's edge using pins or non-toxic craft glue.

SUGAR BALLS AND DRAGÉES

2 These delightful sugar balls can be purchased in edible metallic gold, silver and a coloured pearl effect in various sizes. Larger and in-between sizes can be made by simply rolling balls of white flowerpaste or flowerpaste mixed with sugarpaste and then sprayed gold or dipped into edible gold, silver or pearl petal dusts to create the desired effect (here I used antique gold and pearl). The gold and silver commercially available dragées can also be cleaned off with a little water or clear alcohol leaving a white ball which can then be re-coloured.

3 Attach the antique gold and pearl-effect balls/dragées in clusters dotted around the edges of the cake and drum using small dots of lilac royal icing piped through a No.1 piping tube. Add piped lilac royal iced trailing dots to soften the edges of each cluster using the same piping tube. Leave to dry.

4 Dilute some African violet and white petal dusts with a little clear alcohol to paint small petals around the edges of each cluster of balls. Repeat using plum petal dust to add some pink petals too.

SPRAY ASSEMBLY

5 Use half-width nile green floristry tape to bind together the flowers and foliage, using the large orchid as the focal point. Add trails of coloured paper-covered wires to elongate the display and then tape in smaller groups of flowers and foliage at intervals down the length of the trailing wires. Insert the handle of the spray into a posy pick and then insert it into the cake, trailing the length around the side of the cake.

80th birthday

This brightly coloured rose and lavender display was designed as a feminine 80th birthday cake. However, it could be used to celebrate any other milestone age or even as a single-tired wedding cake. The piped leaf side design is very easy to execute and creates an unusual, yet very effective, finish to the design.

MATERIALS

23 cm (9 in) round rich fruitcake placed on a thin cake board of the same size

1 kg (2 lb 3 oz) white almond paste

1.5 kg (3 lb 5 oz) white sugarpaste coloured with gooseberry paste food colour

Lavender braid

Royal icing

Lavender velvet ribbon

Pins or non-toxic craft glue stick (Pritt)

Gooseberry paste food colour

Pearlised dragées

African violet, white bridal satin, plum and gold petal dusts

Clear alcohol (Cointreau or kirsch)

Nile green floristry tape

Food-grade plastic posy pick

EQUIPMENT

33 cm (13 in) round thick cake drum

Piping bag fitted with a leaf tube

Piping bag fitted with a No.1 plain tube

Fine paintbrush

FLOWERS

10 pink roses of varying sizes (p 32–5)

7 epigenium orchids (p 52–4)

12 green beetleweed leaves (p 106)

15 sprigs of French lavender (p 56–7)

7 trails of hearts entangled (p 26)

PREPARATION

1 Cover the cake and cake drum as described on p 16–7. Transfer the cake onto the cake drum and allow to dry at least overnight before piping the side design. Attach a band of lavender braid around the base of the cake, using a dab of royal icing or softened sugarpaste to hold it in place. Secure a band of lavender velvet ribbon to the cake drum's edge using pins or non-toxic craft glue.

PIPED LEAF SIDE DESIGN

2 Colour some royal icing with gooseberry paste food colour to match the depth of colour used in the sugarpaste coating. Fill a piping bag fitted with a leaf tube with a small amount of green royal icing. Pipe a series of leaves onto the side of the cake – you will need to wiggle the bag and tube a little as you pipe to create a little movement to the piped leaves. Allow to dry before continuing.

3 Next, fill a piping bag fitted with a No.1 plain tube with green royal icing. Carefully pipe a dot of royal icing above each leaf to secure a single dragée onto each one. Use the same tube to pipe a leaf shape onto either side of the dragée. If the larger leaf shape is dry enough you can now continue to pipe tiny dots onto the edge of

each leaf. Allow to dry before painting the dragées with a diluted mixture of African violet, white bridal satin and clear alcohol. Use this colouring and a fine paintbrush to highlight the piped dots on the edges of the leaves too. Dilute a small amount of plum petal dust and add extra painted leaf detail above the dragées and use a tiny amount of diluted gold petal dust at the very tip of each of the ornate piped leaves.

4 Assemble the larger posy using the largest rose as the focal flower. Add the other flowers and foliage around this central flower to create a rounded posy-style shape using half-width nile green floristry tape to hold them in place. Soften the edges of the posy using the hearts entangled foliage to twine around the display. Insert the handle of the posy into the posy pick and insert this into the cake. Tape together a smaller spray, again using a rose as the focal point and add the remaining sprigs of flowers and foliage to create a slightly tapered display. Rest this spray at the base of the cake to complete the design.

Silver anniversary

The exotic white bombax flowers, purple-tinged fern, purple chillies and lilac crown this 25th wedding anniversary cake. The silver fern leaves made from sugar and edible silver leaf remind me of the silver paper leaves so often used in old-fashioned cake decorating books. I guess everything must come full circle!

1 Cover both the dummy cake and the fruitcake, as well as the cake drum as described on p 16–7 (but leave off the white almond paste covering on the dummy cake). Leave to dry for several days. I usually use a dummy cake whenever I have such an extreme tilt in a display – it stops me worrying about it collapsing! Attach a band of fine lavender ribbon around the base of both cakes, using a dab of royal icing or softened sugarpaste to keep it in place. Secure a band or broad lavender velvet ribbon to the cake drum's edge using pins or non-toxic craft glue.

2 Insert three clear plastic dowels into the base tier to support the angle of the dummy cake. Position the dummy cake on top.

3 Cut out some edible silver leaf-covered flowerpaste fern leaves using the three sizes of Australian fern cutters (see p 19 for more information). Dilute some African violet and white bridal satin petal dusts with clear alcohol and paint a series of dots to soften the edge of the design. Add fine foliage and vine green lines.

4 Use half-width nile green floristry tape to assemble the two sprays. For the larger spray, start with the bombax flower to create the focal point, adding the other flowers and foliage to it to create an almost 'S'-shaped spray. Insert the large spray into a posy pick and then into the top tier. The smaller spray is a simple group of each of the elements used in the larger spray (minus a bombax flower). Rest the small spray against the cake drum. Thread some fine crimped wire through several crystal droplets and tie at intervals into the floral displays.

Pearl anniversary

This pretty two-tiered 30th pearl anniversary cake features pearlised sugar dragées and a bouquet of pretty green and pink orchids. This cake could also serve as a wedding cake.

MATERIALS

15 cm (6 in) curved heart dummy cake
25 cm (10 in) curved heart rich fruitcake placed on a thin cake board of the same size
Silver cake board paper
1.25 kg (2 lb 10 oz) white almond paste
1.4 kg (3 lb) white sugarpaste coloured with gooseberry green paste food colour
Green floral ribbon
Royal icing
Large corsage pins
Gold organza material
Pearl dragées in various sizes (APOC)
Edible gold/silver leaf-covered flowerpaste
White bridal satin, plum, African violet and green lustre petal dusts
Clear alcohol (Cointreau or kirsch)
Green paper-covered wire
Nile green floristry tape
Gold wire

EQUIPMENT

Tall tilting cake stand (CC)
Piping bag fitted with a No.1 piping tube
Fine paintbrush
Tall glass bottle

FLOWERS

3 stems of Vincent orchids (p 67)
5 moth orchids (p 64–6)
5 epigenium orchids (p 52–4)
3 pachyveria succulents (p 29)
10 trails of hearts entangled (p 26)

I prefer to use a dummy cake for the extreme tilt of the top tier as it is lighter than a real cake. The bottom tier is a real fruitcake and is displayed at less of a tilt. Cake boards for this shape are not commercially available so it is a case of finding a kind soul to cut the boards for you and then cover them with silver cake board paper. Cover both the dummy cake and the fruitcake as described on p 16 (but leave off the white almond paste covering on the dummy cake).

1 Attach a band of green floral ribbon around the base of each cake, using a dab of royal icing or softened sugarpaste to hold it in place. Alternatively, wet the ribbon, remove the excess water and then wrap it around the cake – this makes the ribbon sticky and adheres the two together. The ribbon eventually dries to an even colour.

2 Position the smaller dummy cake onto the tilting cake stand using large corsage pins to hold it in place. Wrap some gold organza material around the stand and pin this into the base of the cake too.

3 Attach the various sizes of pearl dragées in groups around the curve of each cake, using small piped dots of royal icing to secure them. The flakes of gold and silver leaf are simply leftover pieces of gold and silver leaf-coated flowerpaste from other

projects (see p 19 for more information) that were broken up to leave shards that are ideal for adding interest to a design. Attach these too with royal icing.

4 Dilute some white bridal satin, plum and African violet petal dusts with clear alcohol and paint over some of the dragées. Do the same with the green lustre petal dust and then add painted dotted lines to connect the dragées groups together.

5 Form the outline of the bouquet by plaiting several lengths of green paper-covered wire – try not to make the end result too neat. Curve the plaits into almost a heart shape. Add a tangled ball of green paper-covered wire at the centre of the heart shape: this will bulk up the focal area. Next, tape in the three stems of Vincent orchids, following the heart outline of the bouquet using half-width nile green floristry tape. Use the moth orchids at the centre of the display to create the focal point; these should stand slightly higher than any of the other flowers in the bouquet. Add the epigenium orchids to fill in around the moth orchids. Finally, add the pachyveria succulents, trails of hearts entangled and lengths of curled gold wire to complete the bouquet. Position the bouquet behind the cakes displayed in a glass bottle and draped with more gold organza.

Ruby anniversary

Rice paper is a great medium to cut out as a quick and effective decoration on a celebration cake, adding a nice gentle texture to a design. The rice paper can also be coloured with petal dust or painted with melted cocoa butter to add extra interest.

1 Cover the cake and cake drum as described on p 16–7. Attach a band of fine ruby red ribbon around the base of the cake using a dab of royal icing or softened sugarpaste to hold it in place. Secure a band of broader ruby red ribbon to the cake drum's edge using pins or non-toxic craft glue.

RICE PAPER SPIRALS

2 Use a spiral paper punch to cut out several shapes from sheets of pale pink rice paper. These shapes can be attached to the cake with grated cocoa butter melted over a mug of just-boiled water, or clear piping gel, or simply placed against the cake, as I have done here. I have alternated their positions and also reversed the sides of the rice paper to show both the lined and smooth textures of the paper.

3 Melt some grated cocoa butter onto a dish above a mug filled with just-boiled water. Mix some plum petal dust with a touch of African violet. Paint in extra details. Add foliage green and aubergine spots to complete the design.

FLORAL DISPLAY

4 The centre of the display is made from a tangled ball of coloured paper-covered wires. The flowers are then pulled through the ball to complete the design. Use the old-fashioned rose recessed behind the degarmoara orchids which form the focal point of the spray, taping them all together to form a handle using half-width nile green floristry tape. Soften the edges with the oxalis flowers and foliage. Fill in any gaps with red beetleweed leaves and other assorted foliage.

5 Thread several red and purple beads onto lengths of purple and deep magenta crimped wires, twisting the wires together to hold the beads' position. Thread the beaded wire through the spray and create a trail to hang over the side of the cake. Insert the handle of the spray into a posy pick pushed into the cake.

Gardener's retirement

This unusual cake with its fruit, vegetable and flower combination, would make
an ideal birthday cake design for anyone passionate about plants;
it would make a wonderful retirement cake too!

PREPARATION

1 Cover the cake and cake drum as described on p 16–7. Transfer the cake on top of the cake drum and allow to dry at least overnight. Attach a band of dusky pink ribbon around the base of the cake, using a dab of royal icing or softened sugarpaste to hold it in place. Secure a band of dark red velvet ribbon to the cake drum's edge using pins or non-toxic craft glue.

RADISH SIDE DESIGN

2 Melt some grated cocoa butter onto a dish above a mug filled with just-boiled water. Mix in the various petal dusts to create the paints to execute the radish design: use plum and white petal dusts to create the main body of the radish and foliage mixed with white for the leaves. Define the shapes by outlining with aubergine petal dust mixed into the colours. I painted these freehand but you might prefer to trace the designs on p 142 and scribe them onto the surface of the cake using a scriber or a pen that has run dry. Allow each colour to set slightly before adding darker colour and defining lines.

3 Create a tangled ball of coloured paper-covered wires to form the bulk behind the focal point of the bouquet. Twist several lengths of the same colours of paper-covered wire to add a trail which needs to be threaded into the tangled ball of wire. Next, thread the clematis flower through the centre of the wire ball to create the focal point. Add the clematis foliage to trail and twine around the wire trail. Keep adding the chillies, rose hips and beetleweed foliage around the clematis to fill in the bouquet, taping them onto the clematis stem with half-width nile green floristry tape – this will form the handle of the bouquet. Tie the radish into bundles using pink paper-covered wire and then thread and tape these into place. Add the oxalis flower and foliage at the front of the spray. Finally, thread several groups of the coloured sequins onto the pink crimped wire and thread these at intervals through the bouquet. Insert the handle of the bouquet into a posy pick and then into the cake.

Trick or treat pumpkin

Traditionally, it was the humble turnip, beetroot and apples that were used as symbols for Halloween. We have the early settlers in America to thank for the introduction of the colourful and much easier to carve pumpkin. This pumpkin cake was quick and great fun to make – the flowers were a much longer process though!

MATERIALS

2 x 600 ml (1 pt) bowl-shaped rich fruitcakes

Apricot glaze

1.5 kg (4 lb) white almond paste

1.5 kg (4 lb) champagne-coloured sugarpaste

Clear alcohol (Cointreau or kirsch)

White flowerpaste

Holly/ivy paste food colour

Dried spaghetti (optional)

Tangerine, coral, foliage, vine, aubergine, nutkin and myrtle bridal satin petal dusts

Edible spray varnish

Nile green floristry tape

Tall orange glass vase

EQUIPMENT

20 cm (8 in) round cake board

Sugarpaste smoother

Palette knife

Small non-stick rolling pin

Celstick

Angled tweezers

Large, flat paintbrush and dusting brushes

23 cm (9 in) round wooden base

FLOWERS

3 orange bombax flowers, plus buds and foliage (p 60–3)

3 stems of Chinese lanterns (p 89–91)

2 trails of clematis foliage (p 80–2)

7 sets of acer foliage (p 93)

10 trails of hearts entangled (p 26)

2 sprigs of hazelnuts, plus foliage (p 84–5)

1 Use metal mixing bowls for baking this shape of cake. You will need to line the bowls with strips of non-stick baking parchment. Remove the cakes from the bowls and trim any excess depth from both cakes to create the required shape. Use apricot glaze to stick the two cakes together and then brush over the whole cake with glaze. Place the cake onto the round cake board prior to coating.

2 Cover the cake with white almond paste. Smooth over the surface with your hands and the sugarpaste smoother. Trim off the excess paste from the base with a palette knife. Next, build up the sections of the pumpkin, rolling large sausage-shaped pieces of almond paste. Attach over the coated cake so that the sections radiate from the centre. Blend and mould each piece as you add them. Indent the top of the pumpkin at the centre using the rounded end of the small non-stick rolling pin and use the celstick to help define the divisions between each of the padded sections.

3 Roll out the champagne sugarpaste not too thinly (you might prefer to colour the paste orange to start with – I decided to build the colour onto the cake using petal dusts in layers to create a more subtle effect).

Moisten the almond paste with clear alcohol and then drape the sugarpaste over the top. Smooth over the paste, gently working it over the padded sections. Trim off the excess at the base and use the celstick and non-stick rolling pin to indent and define the shape of the pumpkin. Use a pad of sugarpaste pressed into the palm of your hand to smooth each section.

4 Mix together some white flowerpaste and sugarpaste to make a firm modelling paste for the stalk. Colour the paste with holly/ivy paste food colour. Roll the paste into a sausage shape and pinch out the base into five points to represent the sepals of the calyx. Pinch several ridges using angled tweezers down the whole length of the stalk. Hollow out the end of the stalk. Twist the whole thing to create an interesting shape. Position the stalk on the indent of the pumpkin. You might prefer to insert dried spaghetti into the stalk to support its weight to keep it upright. Blend each section of the calyx into some of the indents of the pumpkin.

COLOURING

5 It is best to apply layers of petal dust at this stage to achieve strong colouring – leaving the paste to dry will result in much

paler colouring. Use a large, flat paintbrush to apply the colours in layers starting with tangerine then tinges of coral petal dusts. Add a mixture of foliage and vine to tinge one side of the pumpkin. Use aubergine to add shading and depth around the base and in the indents. Use foliage petal dust on the calyx stalk and over-dust with aubergine and nutkin. Use a light dusting of myrtle bridal satin over the whole pumpkin to calm down the colouring a little. Allow to dry and then spray very lightly with edible spray varnish. Place the pumpkin on top of a decorative wooden base.

6 Tape together two bombax flowers using half-width nile green floristry tape; this will form the focal point of the spray. Add two stems of Chinese lanterns to create height. Tape a trailing stem of clematis foliage at the base of the spray. Add the bombax leaves and buds to bulk out the spray. Create interest and soften the edges using the acer foliage and the trailing stems of the hearts entangled foliage. Display the spray in the slender orange glass vase. Tape together the remaining bombax flower, Chinese lantern stem, hazel and trailing foliage to display next to the pumpkin.

Autumn wedding

This beautiful three-tiered wedding cake is adorned with silver leaf hand-painted flowers and floral displays of fiery brassada orchids, acer leaves and twigs of glossy orange ilex berries, creating a very opulent display perfect for an autumn wedding.

MATERIALS

15-cm (6-in), 18-cm (7-in) and 20-cm (8-in) round rich fruit cakes placed on thin cake boards of the same size

1.4 kg (3 lb) white almond paste

1.8 kg (4 lb) white sugarpaste coloured with tangerine paste food colour

Broad brown velvet ribbon

Non-toxic craft glue stick (Pritt)

Pale tangerine-coloured royal icing

White flowerpaste

Edible silver leaf-covered flowerpaste

Tangerine, aubergine and foliage petal dusts

Clear alcohol (Cointreau or kirsch)

Nile green floristry tape

3 food-grade plastic posy picks

EQUIPMENT

33 cm (13 in) round cake drum

Straight-edged sugarpaste smoother

Shallow Perspex separator

Piping bag fitted with a No.1 piping tube

Floral design paper punch

Fine paintbrushes

Fine-nose pliers

FLOWERS

6 brassada orchids (p 86–8)

17 acer leaves (p 93)

11 sprigs of ilex berries (p 92)

1 Cover the cakes and cake drum as described on p 16–7. Place the large cake on top of the coated cake drum and stack the middle tier on top. Blend the edge using the straight-edged sugarpaste smoother. Leave to dry. Secure a band of broad brown velvet ribbon to the cake drum's edge and the sides of the Perspex separator using non-toxic craft glue.

2 Pipe a snail trail around the base of the two bottom tiers using a piping bag fitted with a No.1 piping tube and filled with pale tangerine-coloured royal icing. Next, Place the shallow separator on top of the middle tier and then position the smallest cake on top.

SILVER LEAF SIDE DESIGN

3 Slide the silver leaf-covered flowerpaste (see p 19 for more information) into the decorative paper punch and stamp out the design. Repeat to create enough sections to decorate the sides of the cakes. Use royal icing to attach the sections around the base of the top tier so that each section hangs below the edge of the cake. Attach several pieces to the sides of the other tiers, as illustrated. Leave to dry.

4 Use tangerine petal dust diluted with a little clear alcohol to add detail paintwork to each flower of the design using a fine paintbrush. Continue in the same way, using diluted aubergine petal dust to paint the stems and add a calyx to each section. Paint fine vine leaves onto the surface of the cake using diluted foliage petal dust – this will help to soften the edges of the design.

SPRAY ASSEMBLY

5 Tape together three floral sprays using half-width nile green floristry tape. Insert three posy picks into the required positions and then insert the handle of the spray into them to complete the creation. Curve the stems of flowers and fruit to frame the side of the cake. Re-adjust the floral elements if required using fine-nose pliers.

Christmas celebration

A sugar-frosted white tree is the focal point of this festive cake. I have arranged the flowers and fruit next to the cake to complete the design – however, the tree design also works well by itself if you are short of time!

MATERIALS

20 cm (8 in) elliptical rich fruitcake placed on a thin cake board of the same size

750 g (1½ lb) white almond paste

750 g (1½ lb) white sugarpaste

Clear alcohol (Cointreau or kirsch)

Green velvet ribbon

Royal icing

White flowerpaste

Bridal satin and nutkin petal dusts

Gold dragées

Edible gold leaf-covered flowerpaste

Granulated sugar

Nile green floristry tape

Food-grade plastic posy pick

EQUIPMENT

25 cm (10 in) elliptical decorative base

Sugarpaste smoothers

Non-stick rolling pin

Plain-edge cutting wheel

Fine scissors

Dusting brushes

Circle cutter

Star cutters or rose calyx cutters (OP)

FLOWERS

3 stems of orange chincherinchee (p 95)

10 sprigs of ilex berries (p 92)

7 cucumis fruit (p 94)

5 rose hips (p 36)

1 Cover the cake as described on p 16. Attach the cake to the decorative base using a small amount of sugarpaste softened with a little clear alcohol. Use the sugarpaste smoothers to apply pressure and also blend the paste down onto the base to create a good bond. Attach a band of green velvet ribbon around the base of the cake, using a dab of royal icing or softened sugarpaste to hold it in place. Leave to dry.

FROSTED TREE

2 Mix together equal proportions of white sugarpaste and white flowerpaste. Roll out the paste quite thickly and cut out a freehand tree shape using the plain-edge cutting wheel. Cut into the edges of the tree shape using the plain-edge cutting wheel to create a more feathered edge.

3 Moisten the back of the tree with clear alcohol and place it on top of the cake. Cut into the edges if needed and then cut into the body of the tree with fine scissors. Flick the snipped sections to give more curves to the shape. Use the plain-edge cutting wheel to create a bark texture to the trunk.

4 Dust the tree with bridal satin petal dust and the trunk with nutkin. Embed some gold dragées at intervals in the tree.

5 Cut out some baubles from gold leaf-covered flowerpaste (see p 19 for more information) using the circle cutter, and some stars using either star cutters or rose calyx cutters. Attach the largest star at the top of the tree and the baubles and smaller stars dotted around at intervals.

6 Finally sprinkle the whole tree with granulated sugar to give a frosted finish. Arrange the flowers and fruit into a cresent-shaped spray using half-width nile green floristry tape. Insert a posy pick into the side of the cake and insert the handle of the spray into it. Curve the stems of flowers and fruit to frame the side of the cake.

3

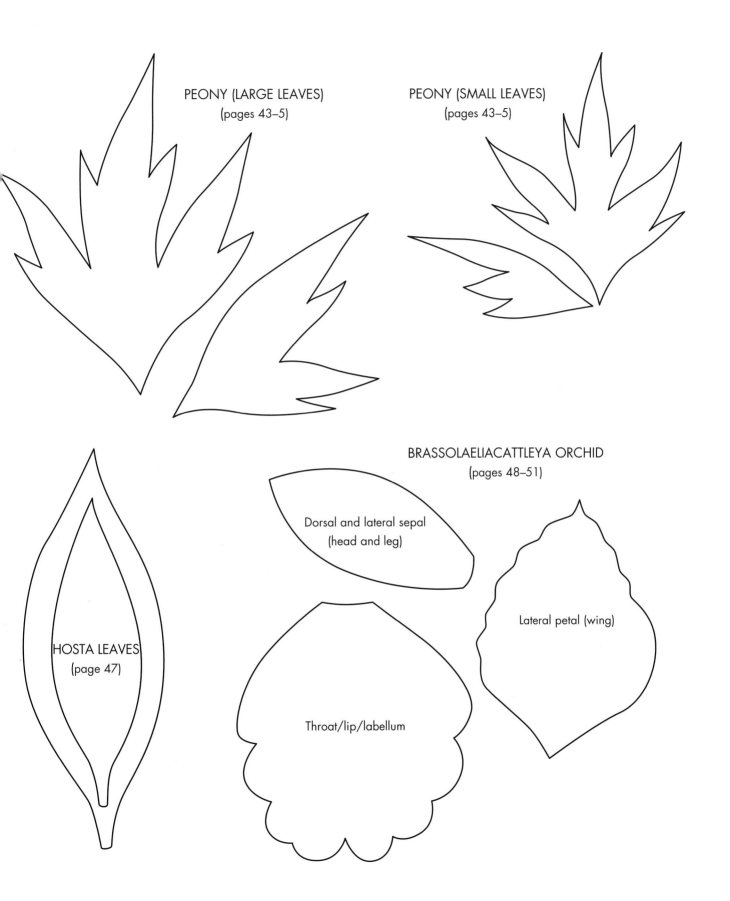

PEONY (LARGE LEAVES)
(pages 43–5)

PEONY (SMALL LEAVES)
(pages 43–5)

BRASSOLAELIACATTLEYA ORCHID
(pages 48–51)

Dorsal and lateral sepal
(head and leg)

Lateral petal (wing)

HOSTA LEAVES
(page 47)

Throat/lip/labellum

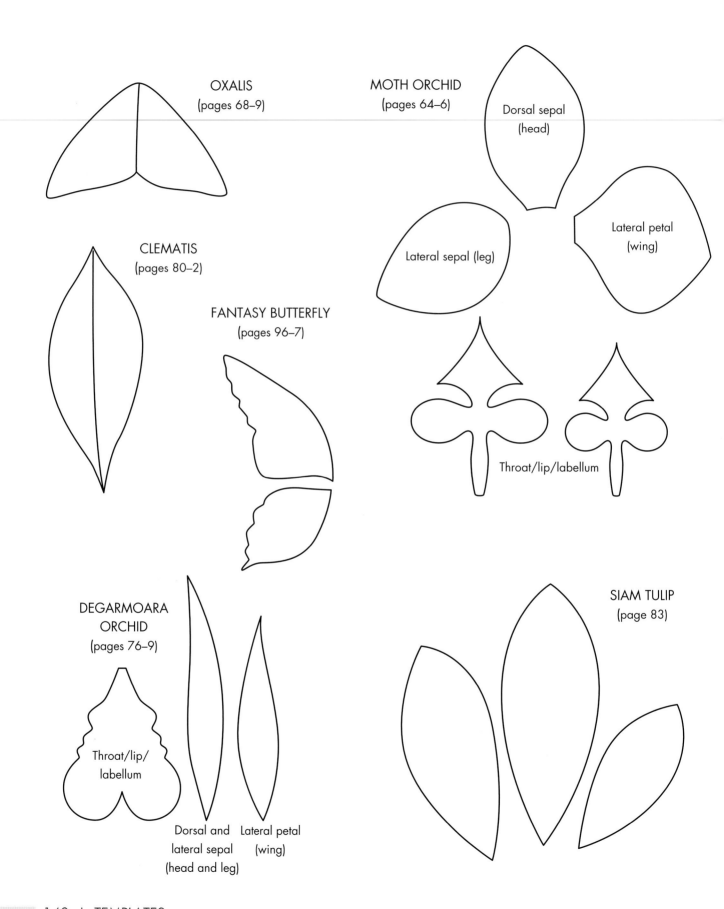

OXALIS
(pages 68–9)

MOTH ORCHID
(pages 64–6)

Dorsal sepal
(head)

Lateral petal
(wing)

Lateral sepal (leg)

CLEMATIS
(pages 80–2)

FANTASY BUTTERFLY
(pages 96–7)

Throat/lip/labellum

DEGARMOARA
ORCHID
(pages 76–9)

SIAM TULIP
(page 83)

Throat/lip/
labellum

Dorsal and
lateral sepal
(head and leg)

Lateral petal
(wing)

BOY'S CHRISTENING
(pages 100–01)

ROSE AND ORCHID
WEDDING
(pages 114–15)

ENGAGEMENT
(pages 112–13)

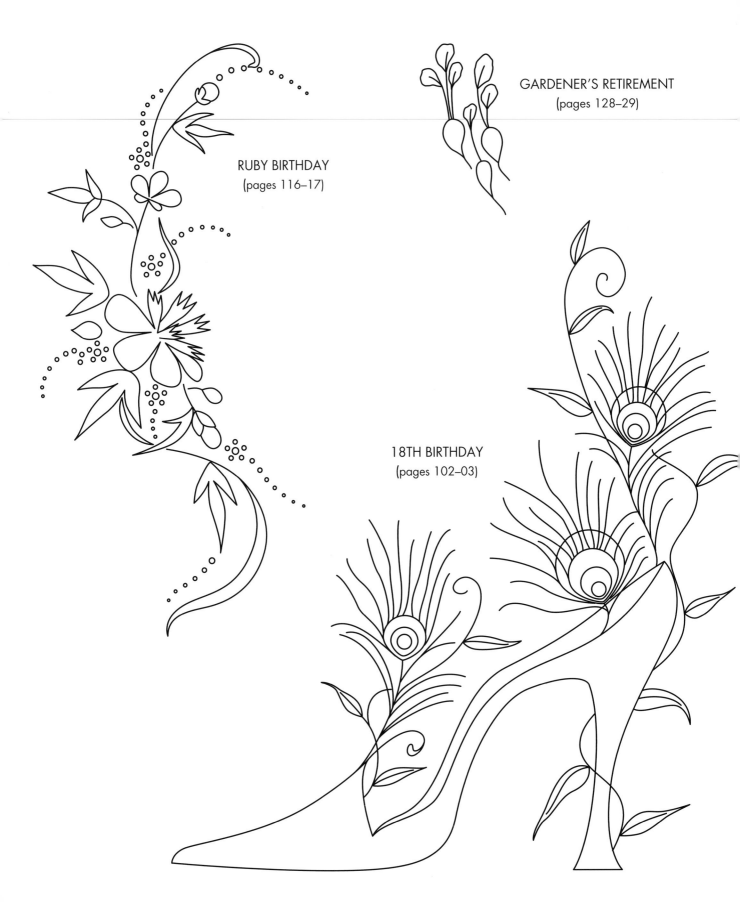

RUBY BIRTHDAY
(pages 116–17)

GARDENER'S RETIREMENT
(pages 128–29)

18TH BIRTHDAY
(pages 102–03)

SUPPLIERS

A Piece of Cake
18 Upper High Street
Thame
Oxon OX9 3EX
www.apieceofcakethame.co.uk

Aldaval Veiners (ALDV)
16 Chibburn Court
Widdrington
Morpeth
Northumberland NE61 5QT
+44 (0)1670 790 995

Cakes, Classes and Cutters
23 Princes Road
Brunton Park
Gosforth
Newcastle-upon-Tyne NE3 5TT
www.cakesclassesandcutters.co.uk

Celcakes and Celcrafts (CC)
Springfield House
Gate Helmsley
York YO4 1NF
www.celcrafts.co.uk

Celebrations
Unit 383 G
Jedburgh Court
Team Valley Trading Estate
Gateshead
Tyne and Wear NE11 0BQ
www.celebrations-teamvalley.co.uk

Culpitt Cake Art
Jubilee Industrial Estate
Ashington
Northumberland NE63 8UG
www.culpitt.com

Design-a-Cake
30/31 Phoenix Road
Crowther Industrial Estate
Washington
Tyne & Wear NE38 0AD
www.design-a-cake.co.uk

Guy, Paul & Co Ltd
(UK distributor for Jem cutters)
Unit 10 The Business Centre
Corinium Industrial estate
Raans Road
Amersham
Buckinghamshire HP6 6EB
www.guypaul.co.uk

Holly Products (HP)
Primrose Cottage
Church Walk
Norton in Hales
Shropshire TF9 4QX
www.hollyproducts.co.uk

Items for Sugarcraft
72 Godstone Road
Kenley
Surrey CR8 5AA
www.itemsforsugarcraft.co.uk

Orchard Products (OPR)
51 Hallyburton Road
Hove
East Sussex BN3 7GP
www.orchardproducts.co.uk

The British Sugarcraft Guild
for more information contact:
Wellington House
Messeter Place
Eltham
London SE9 5DP
www.bsguk.org

The Old Bakery
Kingston St Mary
Taunton
Sommerset TA2 8HW
www.oldbakery.co.uk

Tinkertech Two (TT)
40 Langdon Road
Parkstone
Poole
Dorset BH14 9EH
+44 (0)1202 738 049

Squires Kitchen (SKGI)
Squires House
3 Waverley Lane
Farnham
Surrey GU9 8BB
www.squires-shop.com

Wilton (W) and PME
Knightsbridge Bakeware Centre Ltd
Chadwell Heath Lane
Romford
Essex RM6 4NP

AUSTRALIA
My Cake Delights
219 High Street
Preston 3072
Melbourne
www.mycakedelights.com

Contact the author
www.alandunnsugarcraft.co.uk

Index